THE PHILOSOPHIES OF ASIA

THE EDITED TRANSCRIPTS

ALAN WATTS
at a seminar aboard SS *Vallejo*, 1966

THE
PHILOSOPHIES
OF ASIA

THE EDITED TRANSCRIPTS

Charles E. Tuttle Co., Inc.
Boston ✦ Rutland, Vermont ✦ Tokyo

First paperback edition published in 1999 by Tuttle Publishing, an imprint of
Periplus Editions (HK) Ltd., with editorial offices at 153 Milk Street, Boston,
Massachusetts 02109.

Library of Congress Cataloging-in-Publication Data

Watts, Alan, 1915–1973.
   Philosophies of Asia: the complete edited transcripts / by Alan Watts.
   v. <1>cm.–(Love of wisdom library)
   ISBN 0-8048-3198-X
   1. Philosophy. Oriental. 2. Asia—Religion. I. Title. II.
Series:
B121.W378 1995
181–dc20

                                  95-9751
                                    CIP

Photo courtesy of Alan Watts Electronic Educational Programs

Distributed by

USA
Tuttle Publishing
Distribution Center
Airport Industrial Park
364 Innovation Drive
North Clarendon, VT 05759-9436
Tel: (802) 773-8930
Fax: (802) 773-6993

SOUTHEAST ASIA
Berkeley Books Pte. Ltd.
5 Little Road #08-01
Singapore 536983
Tel: (65) 280-3320
Fax: (65) 280-6290

JAPAN
Tuttle Shokai Ltd.
1-21-13, Seki
Tama-ku, Kawasaki-shi
Kanagawa-ken 214, Japan
Tel: (044) 833-0225
Fax: (044) 822-0413

CANADA
Raincoast Books
8680 Canbie Street
Vancouver, British Columbia
V6P 6M9
Tel: (604) 323-7100
Fax: (604) 323-2600

1 3 5 7 9 10 8 6 4 2   03 02 01 00 99

Design by Frances Kay
Cover design by Jeannet Leendertse
Printed in the United States of America

Dedicated to the memories of
Daisetz T. Suzuki and Christmas Humphreys

*The nub of all these Oriental Philosophies is not an idea,
not a theory, not even a way of behaving, but a way of
experiencing a transformation of everyday consciousness so
that it becomes quite apparent to us that this is the way things are.*

—Alan Watts

CONTENTS

INTRODUCTION

The following chapters constitute the first volume in a collection of literary editions of Alan Watts's classic public lectures. As his son, I spent many hours listening to my father speak, and I often recorded his talks. Years after his death in 1973, I had the opportunity to spend time reviewing all of his tapes, and for this book I have selected some of his most spirited and insightful lectures on Oriental philosophy. *The Philosophies of Asia* is a journey into the spirit of Eastern religious thought. It is at once an introduction and an overview of the primary branches of Oriental philosophy. Most significantly, it is a revelation of the common thread of experience that weaves its way through thousands of years of traditional Asian methods of "teaching the unteachable."

Many of us might ask, "So, why is Eastern thought important today? What is our connection to such foreign and ancient ways of knowing?" Alan Watts answers these questions eloquently in "The Relevance of Oriental Philosophy." This is a powerful public lecture, in which he deals frankly with religion as it is usually practiced in the West and answers important questions about philosophy in general and religious experiences in particular. To Watts the essence of all true religion is the mystical experience, or what is sometimes called God consciousness or cosmic consciousness. He is, however, critical of religious institutions in the West that function primarily as "societies of the saved," whose primary purpose seems to be to distinguish its members from those of the "not-saved."

In the second chapter, "The Mythology Of Hinduism," we explore the world-view of one of the earliest evolving Eastern religious philosophies— that of the ancient Hindus. The cosmology central to religious Hinduism is one in which the godhead is understood to be "dreaming" each of us. This perspective, although radical by Western philosophical standards, is indicative of the unity perceived by the awakened individual. Since the yogic tradition from which both Buddhism and Taoism trace their origins is Indian, a thorough look at Eastern thought begins here, with the philosophy and mythology of Hinduism.

"Eco-Zen" is not an esoteric art form but a down-to-earth look at the Zen of knowing you are one with the world or, as Alan Watts expressed it, feeling the relationship of organism/environment. Speaking before a large college audience, he went on to point out that "ecological awareness" and "mystical experience" are simply two ways of describing the same realization.

"Swallowing a Ball of Hot Iron" examines a means of teaching embodied in the *koan* method of Zen Buddhism. Here the perennial relationship between student and master is explored with great candor. Of course, there are many Zen stories, all of which point toward the inevitable conclusion that, simply put, you are IT.

"Intellectual Yoga" is a profound and often humorous look at the mind as a path to enlightenment. This is one of Alan Watts's later public lectures, delivered in San Francisco in 1971, where we find the mature philosopher performing at ease as he leads us through the tangled web of thinking.

"Introduction to Buddhism" is composed of two seminar sessions recorded aboard Alan Watts's ferryboat home. Here he explains the essential methods and precepts of Buddhism, the difference between the Southern and Northern schools, and the sophistication of Buddha's skills as a psychologist. He then turns to the *bodhisattva* doctrine, the idea of a fully liberated person continuing everyday life "just as it is," to participate in the liberation of all living beings. And finally, he explores the direct method of the Pure Land school of "instant Buddhism."

Finally, we end up with Taoism in "The Taoist Way of Karma." The Taoist ways of dropping out from the chain of *karma* are discussed, as they were recorded in Big Sur, California, during the mid-sixties. We come to "the easy way in" by following the course and current of nature. However, understood this way, nature is not something other than man, as in "man and nature," but the quality of being its self, as in "one's nature."

In translating these stirring speeches onto written pages, I made every attempt to keep the flavor of the original presentation. Certain idiosyncrasies of the spoken form have been removed, and when Alan's thoughts moved more quickly than his words I filled in the blanks—or in the opposite situation, I skipped to the point. In one or two places, dated or currently unfavorable asides were deleted (refer to the audio edition for full flavor), but never at the expense of his desired effect. I trust that you will enjoy reading this first in a series of volumes from a collection of original live recordings by Alan Watts.

—*Mark Watts, 1995*

THE
RELEVANCE OF
ORIENTAL PHILOSOPHY

CHAPTER ONE

Wh-
hen I was a small boy I used to haunt
that section of London around the
British Museum, and one day I came
across a shop that had a notice over
the window which said: "Philosophical Instruments."
Now even as a boy I knew something about philosophy,
but I could not imagine what philosophical instruments
might be. So I went up to the window and there dis-
played were chronometers, slide rules, scales, and all
kinds of what we would now call scientific instruments,
but they were philosophical instruments because science
used to be called natural philosophy. Aristotle once
said that "The beginning of philosophy is wonder."

Philosophy is man's expression of curiosity about everything and his attempt to make sense of the world primarily through his intellect; that is to say, his faculty for thinking. Thinking, of course, is a word used in many ways and is a very vague word for most people. However, I use the word *thinking* in a very precise way. By thinking, as distinct from feeling or emoting or sensing, I mean the manipulation of symbols—whether they be words, numbers, or other signs such as triangles, squares, circles, astrological signs, or whatever. These are symbols, although sometimes symbols are a little bit more concrete and less abstract than that, as in the case of a mythological symbol, like a dragon. However, all these things are symbols, and the manipulation of symbols to represent events going on in the real world is what I call thinking.

Philosophy in the Western sense generally means an exercise of the intellect, and the manipulation of the symbols is very largely an exercise of the intellect, but it does sometimes go beyond that, as in the specific cases of poetry and music. Yet what philosophy has become today in the academic world is something that is extremely restricted. Philosophy in the United States, England, Germany, and France to some extent has fallen into the realm of two other disciplines: mathematical logic on the one hand, and linguistics on the other. The departments of philosophy throughout the academic world have bent over backwards to be as scientific as possible. As William Earl, who is professor of philosophy at Northwestern University, said in an essay called "Notes on the Death of a Culture," "An academic philosopher today must above all things avoid being edifying. He must never stoop to lying awake nights considering problems of the nature of the universe and the destiny of man, because these have largely been dismissed as metaphysical or meaningless questions. A scientific philosopher arrives at his office at nine o'clock in the morning dressed in a business suit carrying a briefcase. He does philosophy until five in the afternoon, at which point he goes home to cocktails and dinner and dismisses the whole matter from his head." Professor Earl adds, "He would wear a white coat to work if he could get away with it."

Of course this critique is a little exaggerated, but by and large this is what departmental academic philosophy has become, and Oriental philosophy is simply not philosophy in that sense. These things, Hinduism, Buddhism, and Taoism, are sometimes also called religions. I question the application of that word to them because I like to use the word religion rather strictly. Now I am not going to be so bold as to venture a definition of religion that is supposed to be true for all time. All I can do is tell you how I use the word, and I wish to use it in an exact sense from its Latin root which really means "a bond or rule of life." Therefore, the most correct use of the word religion is when we say of a man or woman that he or she has "gone into" religion; that is to say, has joined a religious or monastic order and is living under a rule of life or is living a life of obedience.

For if Christianity is a religion, if Judaism is a religion, and if Islam is a religion, they are based on the idea of man's obedient response to a divine revelation. Thus religion, as we understand it in these three forms of religion, consists really of three things we will call the three c's: the creed, the code, and the cult. The creed is the divinely revealed map of the universe or the nature of things. It is the revelation of the existence of God, of Allah, of Yahweh, or as we say, God, by His existence, by His will, and in His design of the universe. That is the creed. To this we add the second c, the code, and this is the divinely revealed law, or exemplar, which man is supposed to follow. In the case of Christianity there is a certain variation in this because the principal revelation of the code in Christianity, as well as the cult, is not so much a law as a person. In Christianity, God is said to be supremely revealed in the historic Jesus of Nazareth. So the code here becomes really the following of Jesus of Nazareth, but not so much an obedience to a law as through the power of divine grace. Then, finally, there is the cult, and this is the divinely revealed method or way of worship by which man relates himself to God through prayers, rites, and sacraments. In these particular religions these methods are not supposed to be so much man's way of worshipping God, as God's way of loving Himself in which man is involved. So, in the Christian religion in the Mass we would say that we worship God with God's own worship, following the saying of that great German mystic, Meister Eckhardt: "The love with which I love God is the same love wherewith God loves me." So, too, when monks in a monastery recite the divine office, the psalms are supposed to be the songs of the Holy Spirit, and so in using the psalms the idea is that you worship God with God's own words, and thereby become a sort of flute through which the divine breath plays.

Now neither Hinduism, Buddhism, nor Taoism can possibly be called religions in this sense, because all three of them significantly lack the virtue of obedience. They do not concede the godhead as related to mankind or to the universe in a monarchical sense. There are various models of the universe which men have used from time to time, and the model that lies behind the Judeo-Christian tradition, if there really is such a thing, is a political model. It borrows the metaphor of the relation of an ancient Near Eastern monarch to his subjects, and he imposes his authority and his will upon his subjects from above by power, whether it be physical power or spiritual power. It is thus that in the Anglican Church, when the priest at morning prayer addresses the throne of grace he says, "Almighty and everlasting God, King of Kings, Lord of Lords, the only ruler of princes, Who dost from Thy throne behold all the dwellers upon earth, most heartily we beseech Thee with Thy favor to behold our sovereign majesty, Elizabeth the Queen and all the royal family."

Now, what are these words? This is the language of court flattery, and the title "King of Kings," as a title of God, was borrowed from the Persian emperors. "Lord have mercy upon us," is an image drawn from things earthly and applied to things heavenly. God is the monarch, and therefore between the monarch and the subject there is a certain essential difference of kind, what we might call an ontological difference. God is God, and all those creatures, whether angels or men or other kinds of existence that God has created, are not God. There is this vast metaphysical gulf lying between these two domains. That gives us, as citizens of a democracy, some problems.

As a citizen of the United States you believe that a republic is the best form of government. Yet how can this be maintained if the government of the universe is a monarchy? Surely in that case a monarchy will be the best form of government. Many of the conflicts in our society arise from the fact that although we are running a republic, many of the members of this republic believe (or believe that they ought to believe) that the universe is a monarchy. Therefore, they are, above all, insistent upon obedience to law and order, and if there should be democracy in the Kingdom of God, that would seem to them the most subversive idea ever conceived. Now I am exaggerating this standpoint a little bit just for effect. There are some subtle modifications which one can introduce theologically, but I will not go into them at the moment.

There are at least two other models of the universe which have been highly influential in human history. One is dramatic, where God is not the skillful maker of the world standing above it as its artificer and King, but where God is the actor of the world as an actor of a stage play—the actor who is playing all the parts at once. In essence this is the Hindu model of the universe. Everybody is God in a mask, and of course our own word "person" is from the Latin, *persona:* "That through which comes sound." This word was used for the masks worn by actors in the Greco-Roman theater, which being an open-air theater required a projection of the voice. The word person has, however, in the course of time, come to mean "the real you." In Hindu thought, every individual as a person is a mask; fundamentally this is a mask of the godhead—a mask of a godhead that is the actor behind all parts and the player of all games. That is indefinable for the same reason that you cannot bite your own teeth. You can never get at it for the same reason that you cannot look straight into your own eyes: It is in the middle of everything, the circle whose center is everywhere, and whose circumference is nowhere.

A third model of the universe, which is characteristically Chinese, views the world as an organism, and a world which is an organism has no boss, and even no actor. This is because in any organism there is not really a boss or "top organ." In our culture we are accustomed, of course, to think of our head as ruling the rest of the body, but there could well be an argument about this. I am going to put up a case that the stomach is chief because the stomach, the sort of alimentary tract with a digesting process in it, is surely anterior to brains. There may be some sort of rudimentary nervous system attached to a stomach organization, but the more primitive you are, the more you are a little creature that eats. It is a sort of tube, and in go things at one end and out the other, and because that wears the tube out the tube finds means of reproducing itself to make more tubes so that this process of in and out can be kept up. However, in the course of evolution, at one end of the tube developed a ganglion that eventually developed eyes and ears with a brain in it. So the stomach's point of view is that the brain is the servant of the stomach to help it scrounge around for food. The other argument is this: true, the brain is a later development than the alimentary tract, but the alimentary tract is to the brain as John the Baptist to Jesus Christ, the forerunner of the "big event," and the reason for all the scrounging around is eventually to evolve a brain. Eventually man shall live primarily for the concerns of the brain, that is, for art and science and all forms of culture, and the stomach shall be servant.

Now cynical people, like dialectical materialists, say that this is a lot of hogwash. Really, all history is a matter of economics, and that is a matter of the stomach. It is a big argument, and you cannot decide it because you cannot at this stage have a stomach without a brain or a brain without a stomach. They go together like a back and a front. So, the principle of organism is rather like this: an organism is a differentiated system, but it has no parts. That is to say, the heart is not a *part* of the body in the sense that a distributor is part of an automobile engine. These are not parts in the sense that they are screwed in. When the fetus arises in the womb there are not a lot of mechanics in there lugging in hearts and stomachs and so forth, and fitting them together and screwing them to each other. An organism develops like a crystal in solution or a photographic plate in chemicals. It develops all over at once, and there isn't a boss in it. It all acts together in a strange way and it is a kind of orderly anarchy.

Fundamentally, this is the Chinese view of the world, the principle of organic growth they call *tao,* pronounced "dow." This Chinese word is usually translated as "the course of nature," or "the way," meaning the way it does it, or the process of things. That is again really very different from the Western idea of God the Ruler. Of the tao Lao-tzu says, "The great Tao flows everywhere, both to the left and to the right. It loves and nourishes all things, but does not lord it over them. When merits are accomplished, it lays no claim to them." And so, the Chinese expression for nature becomes a word that we will translate as "of itself so." It is what happens of itself, like when you have hiccoughs. You do not plan to have hiccoughs, it just happens. When your heart beats, you do not plan it; it happens of itself. When you breathe, you cannot pretend that you are breathing. Most of the time you are not thinking about it, and your lungs breathe of themselves. So the whole idea that nature is something happening of itself without a governor is the organic theory of the world.

So, these are the two other theories of nature that we are going to consider in the study of Oriental philosophy: the dramatic theory and the organic theory. I feel that ways of life that use these models are so unlike Christianity, Judaism, or Islam, that we cannot really use the word "religion" to describe these things. Now, what is there in Western culture that resembles the concerns of Buddhism, Hinduism, and Taoism? The trouble is, on the surface, they look alike. In other words, if you go into a Hindu temple or a special Japanese Buddhist temple you will be pretty convinced you are in church (in sort of a Catholic church, at that, because there is incense, chants, bowings, gongs, candles, rosaries, and all the things that one associates with a theistic, monarchical religion). Yet, that is not what is going on. Even though the image of Buddha may be sitting on a throne, covered with a canopy, and royal honors being done, there is no factor of obedience. Probably the nearest thing to these ways of life in the West is, perhaps, psychotherapy in some form, although not all forms of psychotherapy. The objective of psychotherapy is, as you might say, to change your state of consciousness. If you, in other words, are horribly depressed and you are terrified, or if you are having hallucinations, you see a "head shrinker" and he tries to change your state of consciousness.

Fundamentally, these Oriental disciplines are concerned basically with changing your state of consciousness. However, here we part company because psychotherapy is largely focused on the problems of the individual as such, the problems particular to this individual or that individual. Instead, these Asian ways of life are focused on certain problems peculiar to man as such, and to every individual on the understanding that the average human being (and the more civilized he is the more this is true) is hallucinating. The average human being has a delusive sense of his own existence, and it is thus that the very word "Buddha," in Buddhism, is from a root in Sanskrit, *buddh,* which means to awaken.

To awaken from the illusion is then to undergo a radical change of consciousness with regard to one's own existence. It is to cease being under the impression that you are just "poor little me," and to realize who you really are, or *what* you really are behind the mask.

But there is a difficulty in this. You can never get to see what the basic self is. It is always and forever elusive.

And so, if I ask you, "Who are you really?" And you say, "Well, I am John Doe." "Oh? Ha-ha! You think so? John Doe, tell me: How do you happen to have blue eyes?" "Well," you say, "I do not know. I did not make my eyes." "Oh, you didn't? Who else?" "Well, I have no idea how it is done."

"You have to have an idea how it is done to be able to do it? After all, you can open and close your hand perfectly easily. And you say, 'I know how to open my hand. I know how to close my hand because I can do it.' But *how* do you do it?"

"I do not know. I am not a physiologist."

"A physiologist says he knows how he does it, but he cannot do it any better than you can. So, you are opening and closing your hand, are you not? Yet you do not know how you do it. Maybe you are 'blue-ing' your eyes, too! You do not know how you do it, because when you say 'I do not know how I do it,' all you are saying is, 'I do know *how* to do it, but I cannot put it into words!'"

I cannot, in other words, translate the activity called "opening and closing my hand" into an exact system of symbols, that is, into thinking. If you actually could translate the opening and closing of your hand into an exact system of symbols, it would take forever because trying to understand the world purely by thinking about it is as clumsy a process as trying to drink the Pacific Ocean out of a one-pint beer mug. You can only take it one mug at a time, and in thinking about things you can only think one thought at a time. Like writing, thinking is a linear process, one thought after another in a series. You can only think of one thing at a time, but that is too slow for understanding anything at all and much too slow to understand everything. Our sensory input is much more than any kind of one thing at a time, and we respond with a certain aspect of our minds to the total sensory input that is coming in, only we are not consciously aware of it. Nevertheless, you are doing it, but what kind of "you" is this? It certainly is not John Doe. It is not that little ego freak.

There is a lot more to you than you think there is, and that is why the Hindu would say that the real you is the Self, (but with a capital S), the Self of the universe. At that level of one's existence one is not really separate from everything else that is going on. We have something here which I will not call philosophy except in the most ancient sense of basic curiosity. I prefer to call these disciplines *ways of liberation*. These are ways of liberation from maya, and the following of them does not depend on believing in anything, in obeying anything, or on doing any specific rituals (although rituals are included for certain purposes because it is a purely experimental approach to life). This is something like a person who has defective eyesight and is seeing spots and all sorts of illusions, and goes to an ophthalmologist to correct his vision. Buddhism is, therefore, a corrective of psychic vision. It is to be disenthralled by the game of maya. It is not, incidentally, to regard the maya as something evil, but to regard it as a good thing of which one can have too much, and therefore one gets psychic and spiritual indigestion—from which we all suffer.

Now then, I am going to go into the very fundamental guts of Hinduism and certain documents that are known as the *Upanishads*. These documents constitute what is called *Vedanta*, and that is compounded of two words, *veda anta*. *Anta* means "end," or completion or summation, and *Veda* is, of course, related to the Latin *videre*, to see. Veda is the fundamental revelation of the

Hindu way of life contained in its earliest scriptural documents, which are generally dated in the period between 1500 and 1200 B.C. The Upanishads have been the summation of the Veda from over a long period of time, beginning perhaps as early as 800 B.C., although some of the Upanishads are much later than that. However, there is always a doubt in connection with the dating of any Hindu text because unlike the Hebrews, the Hindus have absolutely no sense of history. They view time as circular, as something that just goes round and round again and again, so that what happens today is on the whole very much like what happened yesterday, or a hundred years ago, or a thousand years ago. They view life as a repetitious process of cycles and so there is very little internal evidence in Hindu manuscripts to give us dates between which we can say it must have been written because they were not interested in references to contemporary events. In fact, until relatively recent times, history was little more than keeping chronicles, and the Hindus were less interested in keeping chronicles than the Chinese.

In all there is a great deal of vagueness, and this is compounded by the fact that many of these scriptures were for hundreds of years handed down orally and memorized before being committed to writing. So there is a great deal of vagueness as to how old the tradition is with which we are dealing and it may be earlier or later than the scholars generally suppose. However it seems there was a migration into the Indian subcontinent by peoples from the north who called themselves Aryans, which may have occurred somewhere in the neighborhood of 1500 to 1200 B.C., and they brought with them the faded tradition that merged with whatever aboriginal religions or ways of life that were existing on the subcontinent at that time, and produced the complex which today we call Hinduism. I am not going into the Vedas because they comprise a complicated piece of symbolical interpretation having to do with the rites, the hymns, and the myths of the various so-called gods of the Hindu pantheon. In the philosophy of the Upanishads these gods are seen simply as so many different manifestations of one basic principle, which is called *brahman,* derived from the root *bra,* which means to expand or to grow. Brahman is also called *atman,* or *paramatman,* the supreme self—the "which that which there is no whicher."

The basic position of the Upanishads is that the self is the one and only reality without another, and that all this universe is finally brahman. The universe appears to be a multiplicity of different things and different events only by reason of maya, which is illusion, magic, art, or creative power. Brahman is considered under two aspects: one is called *nirguna,* and the other *saguna.* The word *una* in each case, meaning quality or attribute, and *nir,* being a negative, nirguna is brahman considered without attribute, while saguna is brahman being considered as having attributes. In Christian theology there are exact equivalents to these terms, which you have probably never heard of. The former is called the *apophatic* way of speaking, a Greek term, and the other is the *catophatic.* When a Christian speaks of God as the father, he is speaking catophatically, that is to say by analogy. No theologian in his right mind thinks that God is a cosmic male parent. All a theologian intends to say is God is *like* a father. Even when it is said "God is light," that is still catophatic language. God is like light, but he is not light. The apophatic language states what God is not, so such terms as "eternal," which means nontemporal, infinite, or without limitation, are in this sense negative. When the Hindu speaks most deeply of the ultimate reality of the universe, he applies the phrase *neti, neti,* meaning approximately "no, no," or "not this, not this." In other words, reality—basic reality—eludes all positive conceptualization whatsoever for the very good reason that it is what you are most basically. That is why the Hindu describes in the Vedanta doctrine of the Upanishads the basic energy of the universe as "the unknown." It is never an object of knowledge, and so it is said in the *Kena Upanishad* that if you think that you understand what brahman is, you do not understand. However if you do not understand, then you understand. For the way brahman is known is that brahman is unknown to those who know it, and known to those who know it not. Now that sounds completely illogical, but translated into familiar terms you would say that your head is effective only so long as it does not get in the way of your eyesight. If you see spots in front of your eyes, they interfere with vision. If you hear singing and humming in your ears, you are hear–ing your ears, and that interferes with hearing. An effec-tive ear is inaudible to itself and then it hears everything else. That is just another way of saying the same thing, and when we translate it into sensory terms it is not all paradoxical.

It is basic to Vedanta that brahman, this intangi-ble, nonobjective ground of everything that exists, is identical with the ground of *you.* This is put in the for-mula *tat tvam asi. Tat* is the same as our word "that." *Tvam* is the same as the Latin *tuus,* "thou;" *asi* is "at." We should translate that into a modern American idiom as "You're it." This, of course, is a doctrine that is very difficult for those brought up in the Judeo-Christian tra-ditions to accept, because it is fundamental to Christian and Jewish theology that whatever you are, you are sure-ly *not* the Lord God. Therefore, Christians feel that the

Hindu doctrine—that we are all fundamentally masks of God—is pantheism, and that is a dirty word in Christian theological circles because of the feeling that if everything is God then all moral standards are blown to hell. It means everything is as good as everything else. Since everything that happens is really God, this must include the good things and the bad things, and that seems to them a very dangerous idea. Actually, when viewed from a social perspective, all religious doctrines contain very, very dangerous ideas. However, we will not worry about that for the moment because what the Hindu means by God, when he says Brahman, is not at all the same thing as what a Jew means by the Lord Adonai, because to the Jew and the Christian it means the boss, to whom divine honors are due as above all others. The Hindu, on the other hand, does not mean the boss. He does not mean the King or the Lord as the political ruler of the universe. He means the inmost energy, which, as it were, *dances* this whole universe without the idea of an authority of governing some intractable element that resists his or its power.

If a Christian or a person in a Christian culture announces that he has discovered that he is God, we put him in the loony bin because it is unfashionable to burn people for heresy anymore. However, in India if you announce that you are the Lord God, they say, "Well, of course! How nice that you found out," because *everybody* is. Why then does a great problem arise? Why does it appear that we are *not*? Why do we *think*? Why do we have the sensory impression that this whole universe consists of a vast multiplicity of different things, and we do not see it all as one? Consider though, what do you think it would be like to see it all as one? I know a lot of people who study Oriental philosophy and look into attaining these great states of consciousness, which the

Hindus call *nirvana, moksha,* and what a Zen Buddhist would call liberation or *satori* (their word for enlightenment or awakening). Now what would it be like to have that? How would you feel if you saw everything as really one basic reality? Well, a lot of people think that it would be as if all the outlines and differentiations in the field of vision suddenly became vague and melted away and we saw only a kind of luminous sea of light.

However, rather advisedly, the Vedanta philosophy does not seriously use the word "one" of the supreme self because the word and idea "one" has its opposite "many" on one side, and another opposite, "none," on the other. It is fundamental to Vedanta that the supreme self is neither one nor many, but as they say, non-dual, and they express that in this word *advita.* A is a negative word like *non. Dvita* is from *dva,* same as the Latin *duo,* two. So advita is non-dual. At first this is a difficult conception because naturally, a Western logician would say, "But the non-dual is the opposite of the dual. Therefore, it has an opposite." This is true, but the Hindu is using this term in a special sense. On a flat surface I have only two dimensions in which to operate so that everything drawn in two dimensions has only two dimensions. How, therefore, on a two-dimensional level, can I draw in three dimensions? How, in logic, is it humanly rational to think in terms of a unity of opposites?

All rational discourse is talk about the classification of experiences, of sensations, of notions, and the nature of a class is that it is a box. If a box has an inside, it has to have an outside. "Is you is or is you ain't?" is fundamental to all classifications, and we cannot get out of it. We cannot talk about a class of all classes and make any sense of it. However, on this two-dimensional level, we can create, by using a convention of perspective, the understanding of a third dimension. If I draw a cube, you are trained to see it in three dimensions, but it is still in two. However, we have the understanding that the slanting lines are going out through the back to another square, which is behind the first one, even though we are still on two dimensions. The Hindu understands this term advita as distinct from the term "one" to refer to that dimension. So when you use the word *advita*, you are speaking about something beyond duality, as when you use those slanting lines you are understood to be indicating a third dimension which cannot really be reproduced on a two-dimensional surface. That is the trick.

It is almost as if whatever we see to be different is an explicit difference on the surface covering an implicit unity. Only it is very difficult to talk about what it is that unifies black and white. (Of course, in a way the eyes do. Sound and silence are unified by the ears). If you cannot have one without the other, it is like the north and south poles of a magnet. You cannot have a one-pole magnet. True, the poles are quite different; one is north and the other is south, but it is all one magnet. This is what the Hindu is moving into when he is speaking of the real basis or ground of the universe as being non-dual. Take, for example, the fundamental opposition that I suppose all of us feel, between self and other—I and thou—I and it. There is something that is me; there is an area of my experience that I call *myself*. And there is another area of my experience which I call *not myself*. But you will immediately see that neither one could be realized without the other. You would not know what you meant by *self* unless you experience something other than self. You would not know what you meant by *other* unless you understood self. They go together. They arise at the same time. You do not have first self and then other, or first other and then self; they come together. And this shows the sneaky conspiracy underneath the two, like the magnet between the two different poles. So it is more or less that sort of what-is-not-classifiable (that which lies between all classes). The class of elephants opposite the class of non-elephants has, as it were, the walls of the box joining the two together, just as your skin is an osmotic membrane that joins you to the external world by virtue of all the tubes in it, and the nerve ends, and the way in which the external energies flow through your skin into your insides and vice versa.

But we do see and feel and sense—or at least we think we do—that the world is divided into a great multiplicity. A lot of people would think of it as a collection of different things, a kind of cosmic flotsam and jetsam washed together in this particular area of space, and prefer to take a pluralistic attitude and not see anything underlying. In fact, in contemporary logical philosophy, the notion of any basic ground or continuum in which all events occur would be considered meaningless for obvious reasons. If I say that every body in this universe—every star, every planet—is moving in a certain direction at a uniform speed, that will be saying nothing at all, unless I can point out some other object with respect to which they are so moving. But since I said the universe, that includes all objects whatsoever. Therefore, I cannot make a meaningful statement about the uniform behavior of everything that is going on. So in the same way that your eardrum is basic to all that you hear, the lens of the eye and retina are basic to all that you see. What is the color of the lens of the eye? We say it has no color; it is transparent in the same way that a mirror has no color of its own, but the mirror is very definitely there, colorless as it may be. The eardrum, unheard as it may be, is very definitely basic to hearing.

The eye, transparent as it may be, is very definitely very basic to seeing. So therefore, if there were some continuum in which everything that is going on and everything that we experience occurs, we would not notice it. We would not be able, really, to say very much about it except, perhaps, that it was there. It would not make any difference to anything, except for the one all-important difference that if it was not there, there would not be any differences.

But, you see, philosophers these days do not like to think about things like that. It stretches their heads and they would rather preoccupy themselves with more pedestrian matters. But still, you cannot help it; if you are a human being you wonder about things like that. What is it in which everything is happening? What is the ground? Well, you say, "Obviously it is not a *what* because a thing that is a *what* is a classifiable thing." And so, very often the Hindu and the Buddhist will refer to the ultimate reality as *no thing,* not nothing, but no special thing, unclassifiable. You cannot put your finger on it, but it is you. It is what you basically are, what everything basically is, just as the sound of an automobile horn on the radio *is* in one way an automobile horn but basically it is the vibration of the speaker diaphragm. So we are all in the Hindu view "vibrations of the entire cosmic diaphragm." Of course, that is analogy, and I am using catophatic language from the point of Christianity.

The best language is to say nothing but to experience it. The nub of all these Oriental philosophies is not an idea, not a theory, not even a way of behaving, but it is basically a way of experiencing a transformation of everyday consciousness so that it becomes quite apparent to us that that is the way things are. When it happens to you it is very difficult to explain it. So in exactly the same way, when somebody has the sort of break-through that transforms his consciousness (and it happens all over the world, it is not just a Hindu phenomenon), somebody suddenly realizes it is all one, or technically non-dual, and really all this coming and going, all this frantic living and dying—grabbing and struggling, fighting and suffering—all this is like a fantastic phantasmagoria. He sees that, but when he tries to explain it he finds his mouth is not big enough because he cannot get the words out of their dualistic pattern to explain something non-dualistic.

But why is this so? Why are we under this great, magnificent hallucination? Well, the Hindus explain this in saguna language as follows. It is a very nice explanation; a child can understand it. The fact of the matter is the world is a game of hide-and-seek. Peek-a-boo! Now you see it, now you do not, because very obviously if you were the supreme self, what would you do? I mean, would you just sit there and be blissfully one for ever and ever and ever? No, obviously not. You would play games. You would, because the very nature of a no energy system is that it has no energy system unless it lets go of itself. So you would let go of yourself and you would get lost. You would get involved in all sorts of adventures and you would forget who you were, just as when you play a game. And although you are only playing for dimes or chips, you get absorbed in the game.

There is nothing really important to win, nothing really important to lose, and yet it becomes fantastically interesting, who wins and who loses. And so in the same way it is said that the supreme self gets absorbed through ever so many different channels which we call the different beings in the plot, just like an artist or a writer gets completely absorbed in the artistic creation that he is doing, or an actor gets absorbed in the part in the drama. At first we know it is a drama. We go to a play and we say, "It is only a play," and the proscenium arch tells us that what happens behind that arch is not for real, just a show. But the great actor is going to make you forget it is just a show. He is going to have you sitting on the edge of your chair; he is going to have you crying; he is going to have you trembling because he almost persuades you that it is real. What would happen if the very best actor was confronted by the very best audience? Why, they would be taken in completely, and the one would confirm the other.

So, this is the idea of the universe as drama, that the fundamental self, the saguna brahman, plays this game, gets involved in being all of us, and does it so darn well, so superbly acted, that the thing appears to be real. And we are not only sitting on the edge of our chair, but we start to get up and throw things. We join in the drama and it all becomes whatever is going on here, you see? Then, of course, at the end of the drama, because all things have to have an end that have a beginning, the curtain goes down and the actors retire to the greenroom. And there the villain and the hero cease to be villain and hero, and they are just the actors. And then they come out in front of the curtain and they stand in a row, and the audience applauds the villain along with the hero, the villain as having been a good villain and the hero as having been a great hero. The play is over and everybody heaves a sigh of relief: "Well, that was a great show, wasn't it?" So the idea of the greenroom is the same as the nirguna brahman; that behind the whole show there are no differentiations of I and thou, subject and object, good and evil, light and darkness, life and death. But within the sphere of the saguna brahman all these differentiations appear because that is out in front that is on the stage, and no good actor when on the stage performs his own personality. That is what is wrong with movie stars. A person is cast to act a role that corresponds to his alleged personality. But a great actor can assume any personality, male or female, and suddenly convert himself right in front of the audience into somebody who takes you in entirely. But in the greenroom he is his usual self. So Hinduism has the idea that as all the conventions of drama go right along with it, that all this world is a big act, *lila,* the play of the supreme self, and is therefore compared to a dream—to a passing illusion, and you should not, therefore, take it seriously. You may take it sincerely, perhaps, as an actor may be sincere in his acting, but not seriously, because that means it throws you for a loop (although that, of course is involved). We do take it seriously. But, this is one of the great questions you have to ask yourself when you really get down to the nitty-gritty about your own inmost core: Are you serious, or do you know deep within you that you are a put-on?

THE
MYTHOLOGY OF
HINDUISM

CHAPTER TWO

I want to start out by explaining quite carefully what I mean by mythology. The word is very largely used to mean fantasy, or something that is definitely not fact, and it's used therefore in a pejorative, or put-down, sense. So that when you call something a mythology or a myth, it means you don't think much of it. But the word is used by philosophers and scholars in quite another sense, where to speak in the language of myth is to speak in images rather than to speak in what you might call plain language, or descriptive language. You can sometimes say more things with images than you can say with concepts. As a matter of fact, images are really at the root of thinking. One of the basic ways in which we think is by analogy. We think that the life of human beings might be compared to the seasons of the year. Now, there are many important differences between a human life and the cycle of the seasons, but nevertheless, one talks about the winter of life and the spring of life, and so the image becomes something that is powerful in our thinking. Furthermore, when we try to think philosophically in abstract concepts about the nature of the universe, we often do some very weird things. It is considered nowadays naive to think of God as an old gentleman with a long white beard who sits on a golden throne and is surrounded with winged angels. We say, "Now, no sensible person could possibly believe that God is just like that." Therefore, if you become more sophisticated and you follow Saint Thomas Aquinas, you think of God as "necessary being." If you think with Buddhists you think of God as the undifferentiated void, or as the infinite essence. But actually, however rarefied those concepts sound, they are just as anthropomorphic, that is to say, just as human and in the form of the human mind, as the picture of God as the old gentleman with the white beard, or as d'Lord in the old television show *Green Pastures*, wearing a top hat and smoking a cigar.

All ideas about the world, whether they be religious, philosophical, or scientific, are translations of the physical world and of worlds beyond the physical into the terms and shapes of the human mind. There is no such thing as a nonanthropomorphic idea. The advantage of d'Lord in talking about these things is that nobody takes it quite seriously, whereas the undifferentiated aesthetic continuum could be taken seriously. That would be a great mistake, because you would think you understood what the ultimate reality is. So, I am going to use very largely naive mythological terms to discuss these matters. If you are a devout Christian, you must not be offended by this. You will naturally think that you have risen now to a more superior idea of these things than these very simple terms derived from the imagery of the Bible and the medieval church. I shall discuss Hinduism in the same way, and I am going to begin with Hinduism to give you a sort of fundamental account of what it is all about.

I imagine some of you were present at the lecture I gave in the university on religion and art, in which I discussed the view of the world as drama. Now I want to go more thoroughly into this, because the Hindu view of the universe is fundamentally based on the idea of drama, that is to say, of an actor playing parts. The basic actor in this drama is called *Brahma*, and this word comes from the Sanskrit root *bra,* which means "to swell or expand." The Hindu idea of Brahma, the Supreme Being, is linked with the idea of the self. In you, deep down you feel that there is what you call "I," and when you say "I am," that in Sanskrit is *aham.* And everybody, when asked what his name is, replies, "I am I. I am I, myself." So, there is the thought that in all life, the self is the fundamental thing; it means the center. The Brahma is looked upon as the self and the center of the whole universe, and the fundamental idea is that there is only one self. Each one of us is that self, only it radiates like a sun or a star. So, just as the sun has innumerable rays, or just as you can focus the whole sun through a magnifying glass and concentrate it on one point, or as an octopus has many tentacles, or as a sow has many tits, so, in these ways, Brahma is wearing all faces that exist, and they are all the masks of Brahma. They are not only human faces but also animal faces, insect faces, vegetable faces, and mineral faces; everything is the supreme self playing at being that.

The fundamental process of reality is, according to the Hindu myth, hide-and-seek, or lost and found. That is the basis of all games. When you start to play with a baby, you take out a book and you hide your face behind it. Then you peek out at the baby, and then you peek out the other way, and the baby begins to giggle, because a baby, being near to the origins of things, knows intuitively that hide-and-seek is the basis of it all. Children like to sit in a high chair, to have something on the tray, and "make it gone." Then somebody picks it up and puts it back, and they make it gone again.

Now then, that is a very sensible arrangement. It is called in Sanskrit *lila,* and that means "sport" or "play," but the play is hide-and-seek. Now, let's go a little bit into the nature of hide-and-seek. I don't want to insult your intelligence by telling you some of the most elementary things that exist, but, really, everything is a question of appearing and disappearing. For example, if I sit next to the object of my desire and I put my hand on the person's knee and leave it there, after a while they will cease to notice it. But if I gently pat them on the knee because now I'm there and now I'm not, it will be more noticeable. So, all reality is a matter of coming and going. It is vibration, like a wave of positive and negative electricity. It is up and down, and things like wood appear to be solid, much in the same way that the blades of a fast-moving electric fan appear to be solid. So, the vast agitation that is going on in the electrical structure of solid things is a terrific agitation that will not allow the agitation called my hand to go through it.

Other kinds of agitation, like X rays, are so constructed that they can get through. So, everything is basically coming and going. Take, for example, sound. If you listen to sound and slow the sound down, just as when you look with a magnifying glass you find that solid things are full of holes, when you magnify sound you find it is full of silences. Sound is sound-silence. There is no such thing as pure sound, just as there is no such thing as pure something—something always goes together with nothing. Solids are always found in spaces, and no spaces are found except where there are solids. You might imagine there being a space without any solid in it, but you will never, never encounter one, because you will be there in the form of a solid to find out about it. They go together, these things, solid and space. The positive and the negative and the "here we are and here we aren't" all go together in the same way, like the back and front of a coin. You can't have a coin that has a back and no front. The only thing that gets anywhere near that is a Möbius strip, which is a mathematical construct in which the back and the front are the same, but that only shows in a more vivid way how backs and fronts go together. So, the whole thing is based on that.

Now, once we have this game there are two different things, but they are really the same. The Brahma is what is basic, but the Brahma manifests itself in what are called the *dvanva*, and that makes the pairs of opposites (duality). *Dva* is the Sanskrit word for "two," which becomes *duo* in Latin and *dual* in English. Two is the basis, and you cannot go behind two, because one has an opposite; the opposite of one is none. Now, what is in common between one and none? No one can say— you can't mention it. It is called Brahma, and it is sometimes called *om*. Yet you can't really think of what is in common between black and white, because there is obviously a conspiracy between black and white; they are always found together. Tweedledee and Tweedledum agreed to have a battle, and there is always an agreement underlying this difference; that is what we call implicit, but the difference is explicit. So, the first step in what you might call the hide phase of the game of hide-and-seek is to lose sight of the implicit unity between black and white, yes and no, and existence and nonexistence.

Losing sight of the fundamental unity is called *maya,* a word that means many things, but primarily it means "creative power," or "magic," and also "illusion"—the illusion that the opposites are really separate from each other. Once you think that they are really separate from each other you can have a very thrilling game. The game is, "Oh dear, black might win," or "We must be quite sure that white wins." Now, which one ought to win? When you look at this page, you would say the reality here is the writing; that is what is significant. Yet there are many other patterns that you can find in which you are undecided in your mind as to which is the figure and which is the background. It could be a black design on a white sheet, or it could be a white design on a black sheet, and the universe is very much like that. Space, or the background of things, is not nothing, but people tend to be deceived about this. If I draw a circle, most people, when asked what I have drawn, will say that I have drawn a circle, or a disk, or a ball. Very few people will ever suggest that I have drawn a hole in a wall, because people think of the inside first, rather than thinking of the outside. But actually these two sides go together—you cannot have what is "in here" unless you have what is "out there."

All artists, architects, and people concerned with the organization of space think quite as much about the background behind things and containing things as they do about the things so contained. It is all significant and it is all important, but the game is "Let's pretend that this doesn't exist." So, this is the pretending: "Oh, black might win," or "Oh, white might win." This is the foundation of all the great games that human beings play—of checkers, of chess, and of the simple children's games of hide-and-seek.

It is, of course, the tradition of chess that white gets the first move, because black is the side of the devil. All complications and all possibilities of life lie in this game of black and white. In the beginning of the game, the two pairs are divided, that is to say, dismembered—cut, to separate. In the end of the game, when everything comes together, they are re-membered. To dismember is to hide, or to lose. To remember is to seek and to find. In Hindu mythology, Brahma plays this game through periods of time called *kalpas,* and every kalpa is 4,320,000 years long. For one kalpa he forgets who he is and manifests himself as the great actor of all of us. Then, for another kalpa, he wakes up; he remembers who he is and is at peace. So, the period in which he manifests the worlds is called a *manavantara,* and the period in which he withdraws from the game is called a *pralaya.* These go on and on forever and ever, and it never becomes boring, because the forgetting period makes you forget everything that has happened before. For example, although it inherits genes from the most distant past, each time a baby is born it confronts the world anew and is astonished and surprised at everything. As you get old, you become heavy with memories, like a book that people have written on, as if you were to go on writing on a page and eventually the whole thing were to become black. Then, you would have to take out white chalk and start writing that way. Well, that would be like the change between life and death.

In popular Hinduism, it is believed that each of us contains not only the supreme self—the one ultimate reality, the Brahma, who looks out from all eyes and hears through all ears—but also an individualized self. This self reincarnates from life to life in a sort of progressive or a regressive way, according to your *karma*—the Sanskrit word that means "your doing," from the root *kre,* "to do." There is a time, then, in which we become involved and get more and more tied up in the toils of the world, and are more subject to desire and to passions and to getting ourselves hopelessly out on the limb. Then, there follows a later time when the individual is supposed to withdraw and gradually evolve until he becomes a completely enlightened man, a *mukti*. A mukti is a liberated person who has attained the state called *moksha,* or liberation, where he has found himself. He knows who he is. He knows that he, deep down in himself (and that you, deep down in yourself) are all the one central self, and that this whole apparent differentiation of the one from the other is an immense and glorious illusion.

Now, this is a dramatic idea. In drama, we have a convention of the proscenium arch on the stage and we have a convention of onstage and offstage. There is the curtain, or backdrop, in front of which the actors appear, and behind that there is a dressing room, called the greenroom. In the greenroom, they put on and take off their masks. In Latin the word for the masks worn by the players in classical drama is *persona*. The Latin word *per* means "through," and *sona* means "sound"—that through which the sound comes, because the mask had a megaphone-shaped mouth that would "throw" the sound in an open-air theater. So, dramatis personae, the list of the players in a play, is the list of masks that are going to be worn. Insofar as we now speak about the real self in any human being as the person by inquiring, "Are you a real person?" we have inverted the meaning of the word. We have made the "mask" word mean "the real player underneath," and that shows how deeply involved we are in the illusion. The whole point of a play is for the actor to use his skill to persuade the audience, despite the fact that the audience knows it's at the play, and to have them sitting on the edge of their chairs, weeping or in terror because they think it is real. Of course, the Hindu idea is that the greatest of all players, the master player behind the whole scene, who is putting on the big act called existence, is so good an actor that he takes *himself* in. He is at once the actor and the audience, and he is enchanted by his playing. So, the word maya, or illusion, also means "to be enchanted." Do you know what to be enchanted is? It is to be listening to a chant and to be completely involved in it—or perhaps amazed. What is it to be amazed? It is to be caught in a maze, or spellbound. And how do you get spellbound and what do you spell? You spell words. So, by the ideas we have about the world and through our belief in the reality of different things and events, we are completely carried away and forget altogether who we are.

There is a story about a great sage, Narada, who came to Vishnu. Vishnu is one of the aspects of the godhead, Brahma. Brahma is usually the word given to the creator aspect, Vishnu to the preserving aspect, and Shiva to the destructive aspect. When Narada came to Vishnu and said, "What is the secret of your maya?" Vishnu took him and threw him into a pool. The moment he fell under the water he was born as a princess in a very great family, and went through all the experiences of childhood as a little girl. She finally married a prince from another kingdom and went to live with him in his kingdom. They lived there in tremendous prosperity, with palaces and peacocks, but suddenly there was a war and their kingdom was attacked and utterly destroyed. The prince himself was killed in battle, and he was cremated. As a dutiful wife, the princess was about to throw herself weeping on o the funeral pyre and burn herself in an act of *suttee* or self-sacrifice. But suddenly Narada woke to find himself being pulled out of the pool by his hair by Vishnu, who said, "For whom were you weeping?" So, that is the idea of the whole world being a magical illusion, but done so skillfully—by whom? By you, basically. Not "you" the empirical ego, not "you" who is just a kind of focus of conscious attention with memories that are strung together into what you call "my everyday self." Rather, it is the "you" that is responsible for growing your hair, coloring your eyes, arranging the shape of your bones. The deeply responsible "you" is what is responsible for all this.

So this, then, is in sum the Hindu dramatic idea of the cosmos as an endless hide-and-seek game: now you see it, now you don't. It is saying to everybody, "Of course you worry and are afraid of disease, death, pain, and all that sort of thing. But really, it is all an illusion, so there is nothing to be afraid of." And you think, "Well, but my goodness, supposing when I die there just won't be anything? It will be like going to sleep and never waking up." Isn't that awful, just terrible—nothing, forever? But that doesn't matter. When you go into that period called death, or forgetting, that's just so that you won't remember, because if you did always remember it, it would be a bore. But you are wiser than you know, because you arrange to forget and to die, and keep going in and out of the light. But underneath, at the basis of all this, between black and white, between life and death, is something unmentionable. That's the real you, that's the secret—only you don't give away the show. All of you are now privy to a secret; you are initiates. You know this neat little thing, but you may not have experienced it. You know about it, but you must not give the show away. Don't run out in the streets suddenly and say to everybody, "I'm God," because they won't understand you.

So then, there are people whom we will call far-out. They are far out into the illusion, and they are really lost; they are deeply committed to the human situation. Opposite them are the far-in people, who are in touch with the center.

Now, the very far-out people are to be commended, because they are doing the most adventurous thing. They are lost—they are the explorers and are way out in the jungles. In all societies, in some way or other, the far-out people keep in touch with the far-in people. The far-in people are there—they may be monks, yogis, priests, or philosophers, but they remind the far-out people, "After all, you're not really lost, but it's a great thrill and very brave of you to think that you are." So then, some of the far-in people act as what is called a guru, and the function of a guru is to help you wake up from the dream when your time comes.

In the ordinary life of the primitive Hindu community, there are four castes: the caste of priests, of warriors, of merchants, and of laborers. Every man who belongs to the Hindu community belongs to one of the four castes, which he is born into. That seems to us rather restrictive, because if you were born the son of a university professor you might much prefer to be a waterskiing instructor, and that would mean a shift in caste from what is called the *Brahmana* because the professor in Hindu life would come under the priestly caste. But in a time when there were no schools and everybody received his education from his father, the father considered it a duty to educate the boys, the mother considered it her duty to educate the girls, and there was no choice of a boy being something other than his father. He was apprenticed to him while very young, and the child, as you know, naturally takes an interest in what the parents are doing and tends to want to do it, too.

So, it was based on that, and although it seems

primitive to our way of thinking, that is the way it was. When a man attained the age of maturity in the middle of his life, and had raised a son old enough to take over the family business, he abandoned caste. He became an upper outcast, called a *sannyasi* and he went outside the village, back to the forest. So there are two stages of life: *grihasta,* or "householder," and *vanaprastha,* or "forest dweller." We came out of the forest and we formed civilized villages. The hunters settled down and started agriculture. Then they formed into castes, and every man, as it were, had a function: tinker, tailor, soldier, sailor, rich man, poor man, beggar man, thief—but those are all parts, those are big acts. Who are you really, behind your mask?

So, in the middle of life it is considered up to you to find out who you are. You are going to die in a few years. Before you die, wake up from the illusion so that you won't be afraid of death. When you become vanaprastha you go to a guru, and the guru teaches you yoga, which is the art of waking up. In other words, to remember, as distinct from dismember, is to find out again that our separateness is maya, or in "seeming" only—it is not the fundamental reality. We are all one. Now, how does the guru teach you that? He does it mostly by kidding you. He has a funny look in his eye, as if to say, "Brahma, old boy, you can't fool me." The basic question that all gurus ask their students is, "Who are you?" The great guru of modern times was Sri Ramana Maharshi. Wealthy philosophical ladies from the United States used to go to ask him, "Who was I in my former incarnation?" because they wanted to find out they were Cleopatra, or something like that. He would say, "Who asked the question? Who is it that wants to know? Find out who you are." Well, if you want to find out who you are, you get into a very funny mix-up because it is like trying to bite your teeth. "Who

is it that wants to know who I am? If only I could catch
that thing." And the guru really says, "But now, let's get
going on this, let's concentrate, you see and get that
thing." So, he has people meditating on their own
essence, and all the time he is looking at them with a
funny look in his eye. They think, "Oh dear, that guru,
he knows me through and through. He reads all my
secret and impure thoughts. He realizes my desires and
how badly I concentrate." But really, the guru is laughing himself silly inside, because he sees that this is the
Brahma being quite unwilling to wake up, or not really
ready. Suddenly there comes a shock—the moment when
you realize the truth about that thumb you were catch
ing. You say, "Oh dear, it's, after all, the same hand,"
and there is a shock of recognition. Suddenly you wake
up and exclaim, "Of course!" Now, that moment is
moksha, or liberation. We have many names for it, but
no very clear names. In the West we call it mystical
experience, cosmic consciousness, or something of that
kind. We find it very difficult to express it in our religious language because we would have to say at that
moment, "I have at last discovered that I am the Lord
God." We put people in asylums who discover this, if
this is the way they express it, because it really is for us
the one sure sign of being completely out of your head.
Whereas in India when somebody says "I am the Lord
God," they say, "Well, naturally. Congratulations, at
last you found out."

Our idea of the Lord God, as we shall see, is different from the Hindu idea. You notice that Hindu
images of the divinities usually have many arms, and
that is because they are conceived of as sort of cosmic
centipedes. The centipede does not think how to use
each leg, just as you don't think how to use every nerve
cell in your nervous system. They just seem to use themselves; they work automatically. Well, many things

working automatically together is the Hindu idea of omnipotence, whereas our idea is more technical. The person in supreme control would have to know how he does every single thing. You would ask, "God, how do you create rabbits?" as if he doesn't just pull them out of hats like a stage magician but actually knows in every detail down to the last molecule or subdivision thereof how it is done and could explain it.

Hindus would say that if you ask God, "How do you make a rabbit?" he would say, "That is no problem at all—I just become it." "Well, how do you become it?" "Well, you just do it, like you open your hand or close it. You just do it. You don't have to know how in words." What we mean by understanding and explaining things is being able to put them into words. We do that first by analyzing them into many bits. In the same way, when you want to measure the properties of a curve, which is complicated, in order to say how that curve is shaped, you have to reduce it to tiny points and measure them. So you put a grid of graph paper across, and by telling the position on the graph of where the curve is at every point, you get an accurate description of what that curve is, or how it is, in scientific terms. That is what we mean when we talk about understanding things, but obviously there is another sense of "to understand." You understand how to walk even if you can't explain it, because you can do it. Can you drive a car? Yes. How do you drive a car? If you could put it into words, it might be easier to teach people how to do it in the first place, but one understands and learns many things about driving a car that are never explained in words. You just watch somebody else do it, and you do the same thing.

In this way, then, the Hindu and the Western ideas of God are somewhat different. So, when the Hindu realizes that he is God, and that you are too, he sees the dance of God in everybody all around him in every direction. He does not assume certain things that a Western person might assume if they had the same experience. For example, you know the difference between what you do voluntarily and what happens to you involuntarily. When I see someone else move at the far end of the room, it comes to me with a signal attached to it; that experience is involuntary. When I move, it comes to me with a voluntary signal attached to it. Nevertheless, both experiences are states and changes in my nervous system, but we do not ordinarily realize that. When we see somebody else doing something, we think that it is outside our nervous system. It isn't at all; it is happening in our own brain. Now, if you should discover that it is happening inside you, it might just as well come to you with a voluntary signal attached to it. You could say, "I've got the feeling that I'm doing everything that everybody else is doing. Everything that I see and that I am aware of is my action."

Now, if you misunderstood that, you might think that you were able to control everything that everybody else does, and that you really were God in that kind of technical sense of God. You have to be careful what sort of interpretations you put on these experiences. It is one thing to have an authentic experience of the stars. It is quite another thing to be able to describe accurately their relative positions. It is one thing to have an experience of cosmic consciousness, or liberation, but quite another thing to give a philosophically or scientifically accurate account of it. Yet this experience is the basis of the whole Hindu philosophy. It is as if one comes into the world in the beginning having what Freud called the "oceanic consciousness" of a baby, but the baby does not distinguish, apparently, between experiences of itself and experiences of the external world. Therefore, to the baby, it is all one. Furthermore, a baby has for a long time been part of its mother and has floated in the ocean of the womb. So it has the sense from the beginning of what is really to an enlightened person totally obvious— that the universe is one single organism.

Our social way of bringing up children is to make them concentrate on the bits and to ignore the totality. We point at things, give them names, and say, "Look at that." But children very often ask you what things are, and you realize you do not have names for them. They point out backgrounds, and the shape of spaces between things, and say, "What's that?" You may brush it aside and say, "Well, that's not important. That doesn't have a name." You keep pointing out the significant things to them, and above all what everybody around the child does is to tell the child who he is, and what sort of part he is expected to play—what sort of mask he must wear. I remember very well as a child that I knew I had several different identities, but I knew that I would probably have to settle for one of them; the adult world was pushing me toward a choice. I was one person with my parents at home, another person altogether at my uncle's home, and still quite another person with my own peer group. But society was trying to say, "Now make up your mind as to who you really are." So I would imitate some other child whom I had admired. I would come home and my mother would say, "Alan, that's not you, that's Peter. Be yourself now." Otherwise, you are somehow phony, and the point is not to be phony but to be real.

However, this whole big act is phony, but it is a marvelous act. A genuine person is one who knows he is a big act and does it with complete zip. He is what we would call committed, and yet he is freed by becoming completely committed and knowing that the world is an act. There isn't anybody *doing* it. We like to think things stand behind processes, and that things "do" the processes, but that is just a convention of grammar. We have verbs and nouns, and every noun can obviously be described by a verb. We say "the mat." We can also say "the matting." Likewise, we can say "cating" for "cat." When we want to say, "The cating is sitting," however, we say, "The cat sits," using a noun and a verb—whereas it is all verb; it is all a big act. But remember, you mustn't give the show away.

ECO-ZEN

CHAPTER THREE

I remember a very wise man who used to give lectures like this, and when he came in he used to be silent. He would look at the audience, gaze at everyone there for a particularly long time, and everybody would begin feeling vaguely embarrassed. When he had gazed at them for a long time he would say, "WAKE UP, you're all asleep! And if you don't wake up, I won't give any lecture." Now, in what sense are we asleep? The Buddhist would say that almost all human beings have a phony sense of identity—a delusion, or a hallucination as to who they are. I am terribly interested in this problem of identity. I try to find out what people mean when they say the word I. I think this is one of the most fascinating questions: "Who do you think you are?" Now, what seems to develop is this: most people think that I is a center of sensitivity somewhere inside their skin, and the majority of people feel that it is in their heads. Civilizations in different periods of history have differed about this—Some people feel that they exist in the solar plexus. Other people feel that they exist in the stomach. But in American culture today, and in the Western culture in general, most people feel that they exist in their heads. There is, as it were, a little man sitting inside the center of the skull who has a television screen in front of him that gives him all messages from the eyeballs. He has earphones on that give him all messages from the ears, and he has in front of him a control panel with various dials and buttons, which enable him to influence the arms and legs and to get all sorts of information from the nerve ends. And that is *you*. So, we say in popular speech, "I have a body," not "I am a body." I have one because I am the owner of the body in the same way as I own an automobile. I take the automobile to a mechanic and, occasionally, in the same way, I take my body to the mechanic—the surgeon, the dentist, and the doctor—and have it repaired. It belongs to me, it goes along with me, and I am in it.

For example, a child can ask its mother, "Mom, who would I have been if my father had been someone else?" That seems to be a perfectly simple and logical question for a child to ask, because of the presumption that your parents gave you your body and you were popped into it—maybe at the moment of conception or maybe at the moment of birth—from a repository of souls in Heaven, and your parents simply provided the physical vehicle. So, that age-old idea that is indigenous, especially to the Western world, is that I am something inside a body, and I am not quite sure whether I am or am not my body; there is some doubt about it. I say, "I think, I walk, I talk," but I don't say, "I beat my heart," "I shape my bones," and "I grow my hair." I feel that my heart beating, my hair growing, and my bones shaping is something that happens to me, and I don't know how it is done. But other things I *do,* and I feel quite surely that everything outside my body is quite definitely not me.

There are two kinds of things outside my body. Number one is other people, and they are the same sort of thing that I am, but also they are all little men locked up inside their skins. They are intelligent, have feelings and values, and are capable of love and virtue. Number two is the world that is nonhuman—we call it nature, and that is stupid. It has no mind, it has emotions maybe, like animals, but on the whole it's a pretty grim dog-eat-dog business. When it gets to the geological level, it is as dumb as dumb can be. It is a mechanism, and there is an awful lot of it. That is what we live in the middle of, and the purpose of being human is, we feel, to subjugate nature, and to make it obey our will. We arrived here, and we don't feel that we belong in this world—it is foreign to us: in the words of the poet A.E. Housman, "I, a stranger and afraid, in a world I never made." All around us today we see the signs of man's battle with nature. I am living at the moment in a marvelous house overlooking a lake, and on the other side of the lake the whole hill has suddenly been interrupted with a ghastly gash. They have made level lots for building tract homes of the kind you would build on a flat plain. This is called the conquest of nature, and these houses will eventually fall down the hill because the builders are causing soil erosion and they are being maximally stupid. The proper way to build a house on a hillside is to do it in such a way as to effect the minimum interference with the nature of the hill. After all, the whole point of living in the hills is to live in the hills. There is no point in converting the hills into something flat and then going and living there. You can do that already on the level ground. So, as more people live in the hills, the more they spoil the hills, and they are just the same as people living on the flat ground. How stupid can you get? Well, this is one of the symptoms of our phony sense of identity, of our phony feeling that we are something lonely, locked up in a bag of skin and confronted with a world, an external, alien, foreign world that is not us.

Now, according to certain of these great ancient philosophies, like Buddhism, this sensation of being a separate, lonely individual is a hallucination. It is a hallucination brought about by various causes, the way we are brought up being the chief of them, of course. For example, the main thing that we're all taught in childhood is that we must do that which will only be appreciated if we do it voluntarily. "Now darling, a dutiful child must love its mother. But now, I don't want you to do it because I say so, but because you really want to." Or "You must be free." This also is seen in politics—"Everybody must vote." Imagine, you are members of a democracy, and you must be members of the democracy—you are ordered to. You see, this is crazy. Also "Thou shalt love the Lord thy God." Is that a commandment or a joke? However, if you suggest that the Lord is joking, most people in our culture are offended, because they have a very moronic conception of God as a person totally devoid of humor. But the Lord is highly capable of joking, because joking is one of the most constructive things you can do. So, when you are told who you are, and that you must be free, and furthermore that you must survive, that becomes a kind of compulsion, and you get mixed up. Of course, it is very simple to get mixed up if you think you must do something that will only be required of you if you do it freely.

These are the sort of influences, then, that cause human beings all over the world to feel isolated—to feel that they are centers of awareness locked up in bags of skin. Now, this sensation of our identity can be shown and demonstrated to be false by some of the disciplines of our own science. When we describe a human being or any other living organism from a scientific point of view, all that means is that we are describing it carefully. We are going to describe very carefully what a human being is and what a human being does. We find that as we go on with that description, we can't describe the human being without describing the environment. We cannot say what a human being is doing without also saying what the world around him is doing.

Just imagine for a moment that you couldn't see anything except me. You couldn't see the curtain behind me, or the microphone. You could only see me, and that is all you could see. What would you be looking at? You wouldn't see me at all, because you wouldn't see my edges, and my edges are rather important for seeing me. My edges would be identical with the edge of your eyesight, with that vague oval curve which is the field of vision. What you would be looking at would be my necktie, my nose, my eyes, and so on, but you wouldn't see my edges. You would be confronted with a very strange monster, and you wouldn't know it was a human being. To see me you need to see my background, and therein lies a clue of which we are mostly ignorant. In Buddhist theory, the cause of our phony sense of identity is called *avidya,* meaning "ignorance," although it is better to pronounce it "ig*nor*ance." Having a deluded sense of identity is the result of ignoring certain things. So, when you look at me, I cause you to ignore my background, because I concentrate attention on me, just like a conjurer or stage magician misdirects your attention in order to perform his tricks. He talks to you about his fingers and how empty they are, and he can pull something out of his pocket in plain sight and you don't notice it—and so magic happens. That's ig*nor*ance—selective attention—focusing your consciousness on one thing to the exclusion of many other things. In this way we concentrate on the things—the figures—and we ignore the background. So, we come to think that the figure exists independently of the background, but actually they go together. They go together just as inseparably as backs go with fronts, as positives go with negatives, as ups go with downs, and as life goes with death. You cannot separate it. So there is a sort of secret conspiracy between the figure and the background: They are really one, but they look different. They need each other, just as male needs female, and vice versa. But we are, ordinarily, completely unaware of this.

So then, when a scientist starts carefully paying attention to the behavior of people and things, he discovers that they go together, and that the behavior of the organism is inseparable from the behavior of its environment. So, if I am to describe what I am doing, am I just waving my legs back and forth? No, I am walking. In order to speak about walking, you have to speak about the space in which I am walking—about the floor, about the direction, left or right, in relation to what kind of room, stage, and situation. Obviously, if there isn't a ground underneath me, I cannot very well walk, so the description of what I am doing involves the description of the world. And so, the biologist comes to say that what he is describing is no longer merely the organism and its behavior. He is describing a field, which he now calls the organism/environment, and that field is what the individual actually is. Now, this is very clearly recognized in all sorts of sciences, but the average individual, and indeed the average scientist, does not feel in a way that corresponds to his theory. He still feels as if he were a center of sensitivity locked up inside a bag of skin.

The object of Buddhist discipline, or methods of psychological training, is, as it were, to turn that feeling inside out—to bring about a state of affairs in which the individual feels himself to be everything that there is. The whole cosmos is focused, expressing itself here, and you are the whole cosmos expressing itself there, and there, and there, and there, and so on. In other words, the reality of my self fundamentally is not something inside my skin but everything, and I mean everything, outside my skin, but doing what is my skin and what is inside it. In the same way, when the ocean has a wave on it, the wave is not separate from the ocean. Every wave on the ocean is the whole ocean waving. The ocean waves, and it says, "Yoo-hoo, I'm here. I can wave in many different ways—I can wave this way and that way." So, the ocean of being waves every one of us, and we are its waves, but the wave is fundamentally the ocean. Now, in that way, your sense of identity would be turned inside out. You wouldn't forget who you were—your name and address, your telephone number, your social security number, and what sort of role you are supposed to occupy in society. But you would know that this particular role that you play and this particular personality that you are is superficial, and the real you is all that there is.

SWALLOWING
A BALL OF HOT IRON

CHAPTER FOUR

The inversion, or turning upside down, of the sense of identity, of the state of consciousness that the average person has, is the objective of Buddhistic disciplines. Now, perhaps I can make this clearer to you by going into a little detail as to how these disciplines work. The method of teaching something in Buddhism is rather different from methods of teaching that we use in the Western world. In the Western world, a good teacher is regarded as someone who makes the subject matter easy for the student, a person who explains things cleverly and clearly so you can take a course in mathematics without tears. In the Oriental world, they have an almost exactly opposite conception, and that is that a good teacher is a person who makes you find out something for yourself. In other words, learn to swim by throwing the baby into the water. There is a story used in Zen about how a burglar taught his child how to burgle. He took him one night on a burgling expedition, locked him up in a chest in the house that he was burgling, and left him. The poor little boy was all alone locked up in the chest, and he began to think, "How on earth am I going to get out?" So he suddenly called out, "Fire, fire," and everybody began running all over the place. They heard this shriek coming from inside the chest and they unlocked it, and he rushed out and shot out into the garden. Everybody was in hot pursuit, calling out, "Thief, thief," and as he went by a well he picked up a rock and dropped it into the well. Everybody thought the poor fellow had jumped into the well and committed suicide, and so he got away. He returned home and his father said, "Congratulations, you have learned the art."

William Blake once said, "A fool who persists in his folly will become wise." The method of teaching used by these great Eastern teachers is to make fools persist in their folly, but very rigorously, very consistently, and very hard. Now, having given you the analogy and image, let's go to the specific situation. Supposing you want to study Buddhism under a Zen master—what will happen to you? Well, first of all, let's ask why you would want to do this anyway. I can make the situation fairly universal. It might not be a Zen master that you go to—it might be a Methodist minister, a Catholic priest, or a psychoanalyst. But what's the matter with you? Why do you go? Surely the reason that we all would be seekers is that we feel some disquiet about ourselves. Many of us want to get rid of ourselves. We cannot stand ourselves and so we watch television, go to the

movies, read mystery stories, and join churches in order
to forget ourselves and to merge with something greater
than ourselves. We want to get away from this ridiculous thing locked up in a bag of skin. You may say, "I
have a problem. I hurt, I suffer, and I'm neurotic," or
whatever it is. You go to the teacher and say, "My problem's me. Change me."

Now, if you go to a Zen teacher, he will say,
"Well, I have nothing to teach. There is no problem—
everything's perfectly clear." You think that one over,
and you say, "He's probably being cagey. He's testing
me out to see if I really want to be his student. I know,
according to everybody else who's been through this,
that in order to get this man to take me on I must persist." Do you know the saying, "Anybody who goes to a
psychiatrist ought to have his head examined?" There is
a double take in that saying.

So, in the same way, anybody who goes with a
spiritual problem to a Zen master defines himself as a
nut, and the teacher does everything possible to make
him as nutty as possible. The teacher says, "Quite hon-
estly, I haven't anything to tell you. I don't teach anything—I have no doctrine. I have nothing whatsoever to
sell you." So the student thinks, "My, this is very deep,"
because this nothing that he is talking about, this nothing that he teaches, is what they call in Buddhism *sunyata*. Sunyata is Sanskrit for "nothingness," and it is
supposed to be the ultimate reality. But if you know anything about these doctrines, this does not mean just
"nothing there at all" or just "blank," but it means "no-
thing-ness." It is the transcendental reality behind all
separate and individual things, and that is something
very deep and profound. So, he knows that when the
teacher said, "I have nothing to teach," he meant this
very esoteric no-thing. Well, he might also say then, "If

you have nothing to teach, what are all these students doing around here?" And the teacher says, "They are not doing anything. They are just a lot of stupid people who live here."

He knows again this "stupid" does not mean just straight stupid, but the higher stupidity of people who are humble and do not have intellectual pride. Finally, the student, having gone out of his way to define himself as a damn fool in need of help, has absolutely worked himself into this situation. He has defined himself as a nut, and then the teacher accepts him. The teacher says, "Now, I am going to ask *you* a question. I want to know who you are before your mother and father conceived you. That is to say, you have come to me with a problem, and you have said, 'I have a problem. I want to get one up on this universe.' Now, who is it that wants to get one up? Who are you? Who is this thing called your ego, your soul, your I, your identity, for whom your parents provided a body? Show me that. Furthermore, I'm from Missouri and I don't want any words and I want to be shown."

The student opens his mouth to answer, but the teacher says, "Uh-uh, not yet; you're not ready." Then he takes him back and introduces him to the chief student of all the so-called Zen monks who live there together, and the chief student says, "Now, what we do here is we have a discipline, but the main part of the discipline is meditation. We all sit cross-legged in a row and learn how to breathe and be still: in other words, to do nothing. Now, you mustn't go to sleep and you mustn't fall into a trance. You have to stay wide awake, not think anything, but perfectly do nothing." During meditation, there is a monk walking up and down all the time with a long flat stick, and if you go to sleep or fall into a trance, he hits you on the back. So instead of becoming dreamy, you stay quite clear, and wide awake, but still doing nothing. The idea is that out of the state of profoundly doing nothing, you will be able to tell the teacher who you really are.

In other words, the question "Who are you before your father and mother conceived you?" is a request for an act of perfect sincerity and spontaneity. It is as if I were to ask, "Look now, will you be absolutely genuine with me? No deception please. I want you to do something that expresses you without the slightest deception. No more role-acting, no more playing games with me; I want to see you!" Now, imagine, could you really be that honest with somebody else, especially a spiritual teacher, because you know he looks right through you and sees all your secret thoughts. He knows the very second you have been a little bit phony, and that bugs you. The same is true of a psychiatrist. You might be sitting in there discussing your problems with him and absent-mindedly you start to pick your nose. The psychiatrist suddenly says to you, "Is your finger comfortable there? Do you like that?" And you know your Freudian slip is showing. What do fingers symbolize, and what do nostrils symbolize? Uh-oh. You quickly put your hand down and say, "Oh no, it is nothing, I was just picking my nose." But the analyst says, "Oh really? Then why are you justifying it? Why are you trying to explain it away?" He has you every way you turn. Well, that is the art of psychoanalysis, and in Zen it is the same thing.

When you are challenged to be perfectly genuine, it is like saying to a child, "Now darling, come out here and play, and don't be self-conscious." In other words I could say to you, "If any of you come here tonight at exactly midnight, and put your hands on this stage, you can have granted any wish you want to, provided you don't think of a green elephant." Of course, everybody will come, and they will put their hands here, and they will be very careful not to think about a green elephant. The point is that if we transfer this concept to the dimension of spirituality, where the highest ideal is to be unselfish and to let go of one's self, it is again trying to be unselfish for selfish reasons. You cannot be unselfish by a decision of the will any more than you can decide not to think of a green elephant. There is a story about Confucius, who one day met Lao-tzu, a great Chinese philosopher. Lao-tzu said, "Sir, what is your system?" And Confucius said, "It is charity, love of one's neighbor, and elimination of self-interest." Lao-tzu replied, "Stuff and nonsense. Your elimination of self is a positive manifestation of self. Look at the universe. The stars keep their order, the trees and plants grow upward without exception, and the waters flow. Be like this."

These are all examples of the tricks the master might be playing on you. You came to him with the idea in your mind that you are a separate, independent, isolated individual, and he is simply saying, "Show me this individual." I had a friend who was studying Zen in Japan, and he became pretty desperate to produce the answer of who he really is. On his way to an interview with the master to give an answer to the problem, he noticed a very common sight in Japan, a big bullfrog sitting around in the garden. He swooped this bullfrog up in his hand and dropped it in the sleeve of his kimono. Then he went to the master to give the answer of who he was. He suddenly produced the bullfrog, and the master said, "Mmmmm, too intellectual." In other words, this answer is too contrived. It is too much like Zen. "You have been reading too many books. It is not the genuine thing," the master said. So, after a while, what happens is the student finds that there is absolutely no way of being his true self. Not only is there no way of doing it, there is also no way of doing it by not doing it.

To make this clearer, allow me to put it into Christian terms: "Thou shalt love the Lord, thy God." What are you going to do about that? If you try very hard to love God you may ask yourself, "Why am I doing this?" You will find out you are doing it because you want to be right. After all, the Lord is the master of the universe, and if you don't love him, you're going to be in a pretty sad state. So, you realize you are loving him just because you are afraid of what will happen to you if you don't. And then you think, "That is pretty lousy love, isn't it? That's a bad motivation. I wish I could change that. I wish I could love the Lord out of a genuine heart." But, why do you want to change? You realize that the reason you want to have a different kind of motive is that you have the same motive. So, you say "Oh for heaven's sake, God, I'm a mess. Will you please help me out?" Then he reminds you, "Why are you doing that? Now, you are just giving up, aren't you? You are asking someone else to take over your problem." Suddenly you find you are stuck.

What is called the Zen problem, or koan, is likened to a person who has swallowed a ball of red-hot iron. He cannot gulp it down and he cannot spit it out. Or it is like a mosquito biting an iron bull. It is the nature of a mosquito to bite and it is the nature of an iron bull to be unbiteable. Both go on doing what is their nature, and so, nothing can happen. Soon you realize you are absolutely up against it. There is absolutely no answer to this problem, and no way out. Now, what does that mean? If I cannot do the right thing by doing, and I cannot do the right thing by not doing, what does it mean? It means, of course, that I who essayed to do all this is a hallucination. There is no independent self to be produced. There is no way at all of showing it, because it is not there. When you recover from the illusion and you suddenly wake up, you think, "Whew, what a relief." That is called satori. When this kind of experience happens, you discover that what you are is no longer this sort of isolated center of action and experience locked up in your skin. The teacher has asked you to produce that thing, to show it to him genuine and naked, and you couldn't find it. So, it isn't there, and when you see clearly that it isn't there, you have a new sense of identity. You realize that what you are is the whole world of nature, doing this. Now, that is difficult for many Western people, because it suggests a kind of fatalism. It suggests that the individual is nothing more than the puppet of cosmic forces. However, when your own inner sense of identity changes from being the separate individual to being what the entire cosmos is doing at this place, you become not a puppet but more truly and more expressively an individual than ever. This is the same paradox that the Christian knows in the form, "Whosoever would save his soul shall lose it."

Now, I think that this is something of very great importance to the Western world today. We have developed an immensely powerful technology. We have stronger means of changing the physical universe than have ever existed before. How are we going to use it? A Chinese proverb says that if the wrong man uses the right means, the right means work in the wrong way. Let us assume that our technological knowledge is the right means. What kind of people are going to use this knowledge? Are they going to be people who hate nature and feel alienated from it, or people who love the physical world and feel that the physical world is their own personal body? The whole physical universe, right out to the galaxies, is simply one's extended body. Now, at the moment, the general attitude of our technologists who are exploring space is represented in the phrase "the conquest of space." They are building enormous, shell-like, phallic objects that blast into the sky. This is downright ridiculous, because no one is going to get anywhere in a rocket. It takes a terribly long time to even get to the moon, and it is going to take longer than anybody can live to get outside the solar system, just to begin with. The proper way to study space is not with rockets but with radio astronomy. Instead of exploding with a tough fist at the sky, become more sensitive and develop subtler senses, and everything will come to you. Be more open and be more receptive, and eventually you will develop an instrument that will examine a piece of rock on Mars with greater care than you could if you were holding it in your own hand. Let it come to you.

The whole attitude of using technology as a method of fighting the world will succeed only in destroying the world, as we are doing. We use absurd and uninformed and shortsighted methods of getting rid of insect pests, forcing our fruit and tomatoes to grow, stripping our hills of trees and so on, thinking that this is some kind of progress. Actually, it is turning everything into a junk heap. It is said that Americans, who are in the forefront of technological progress, are materialists. Nothing is further from the truth. American culture is dedicated to the hatred of material and to its transformation into junk. Look at our cities. Do they look as though they were made by people who love material? Everything is made out of ticky-tacky, which is a combination of plaster of paris, papier-mâché and plastic glue, and it comes in any flavor. The important lesson is that technology and its powers must be handled by true materialists. True materialists are people who love material—who cherish wood and stone and wheat and eggs and animals and, above all, the earth—and treat it with a reverence that is due one's own body.

INTELLECTUAL YOGA

CHAPTER FIVE

The word yoga, as most of you doubtless know, is the same as our word *yoke* and the Latin word *jungere,* meaning "to join." *Join, junction, yoke,* and *union*—all these words are basically from the same root. So, likewise, when Jesus said, "My yoke is easy," he was really saying, "My yoga is easy." The word, therefore, basically denotes the state that would be the opposite of what our psychologists call alienation, or what Buddhists call *sakyadrishti,* the view of separateness or the feeling of separateness—the feeling of being cut off from being. Most civilized people do in fact feel that way, because they have a kind of myopic attention focused on their own boundaries and what is inside those boundaries. They identify themselves with the inside and do not realize that you cannot have an inside without an outside. That would seem to be extremely elementary logic, wouldn't it? We could have no sense of being ourselves and of having a personal identity without the contrast of something that is not ourselves—that is to say, other.

However, the fact that we do not realize that self and other go together is the root of an enormous and terrifying anxiety, because what will happen when the inside disappears? What will happen when the so-called I comes to an end, as it seems to? Of course, if it didn't, and if things did not keep moving and changing, appearing and dissolving, the universe would be a colossal bore. Therefore, you are only aware that things are all right for the moment. I hope most of the people in this gathering have a sort of genial sense inside of them that for the time being things are going on more or less okay. Some of you may be very miserable, and then your problem may be just a little different, but it is essentially the same one. But you must realize that the sense of life being fairly all right is inconceivable and unfeelable unless there is way, way, way in the back of your mind the glimmer of a possibility that something absolutely, unspeakably awful might happen. It does not have to happen. Of course, you will die one day, but there always has to be the vague apprehension, the *hintegedanka,* that the awful awfuls are possible. It gives spice to life. Now, these observations are in line with what I am going to discuss: the intellectual approach to yoga.

There are certain basic principal forms of yoga. Most people are familiar with *hatha yoga,* which is a psychophysical exercise system, and this is the one you see demonstrated most on television, because it has visual value. You can see all these exercises of lotus positions and people curling their legs around their necks and doing all sorts of marvelous exercises. The most honest yoga teacher I know is a woman who teaches hatha yoga and does not pretend to be any other kind of guru. She does it very well.

Then there is *bhakti yoga. Bhakti* means "devotion," and I suppose in general you might say that Christianity is a form of bhakti yoga, because it is yoga practiced through extreme reverence and love for some being felt more or less external to oneself who is the representative of the divine.

Then there is *karma yoga. Karma* means "action," and incidentally, that is all it means. It does not mean the law of cause and effect. When we say that something that happens to you is your karma, all we are saying is that it is your own doing. Nobody is in charge of karma except you. Karma yoga is the way of action, of using one's everyday life, one's trade, or an athletic discipline (like sailing or surfing or track running) as your way of yoga, and as your way of discovering who you are.

Then there is *raja yoga.* That is the royal yoga, and that is sometimes also called *kundalini yoga.* It involves very complicated psychic exercises having to do with awakening the serpent power that is supposed to lie at the base of one's spiritual spine and raise it up through certain chakras or centers until it enters into the brain. There is a very profound symbolism involved in that, but I am not going into that.

Mantra yoga is the practice of chanting or humming, either out loud or silently, certain sounds that become supports for contemplation, for what is in Sanskrit called *jnana.* Jnana is the state in which one is clearly awake and aware of the world as it is, as distinct from the world as it is described. In other words, in the state of jnana, you stop thinking. You stop talking to yourself and figuring to yourself and symbolizing to yourself what is going on. You simply are aware of what is and nobody can say what it is, because as Korzybski well said, "The real world is unspeakable." There's a lovely double take in that. But that's jnana, that's *zazen,* where one practices to sit absolutely wide awake with eyes open, without thinking.

That is a very curious state, incidentally. I knew a professor of mathematics at Northwestern University who one day said, "You know, it's amazing how many things there are that aren't so." He was talking about old wives' tales and scientific superstitions, but when you practice jnana, you are amazed how many things there are that aren't so.

When you stop talking to yourself and you are simply aware of what is—that is to say, of what you feel and what you sense—even that is saying too much. You suddenly find that the past and the future have completely disappeared. So also has disappeared the so-called differentiation between the knower and the known, the subject and the object, the feeler and the feeling, the thinker and the thought. They just aren't there because you have to talk to yourself to maintain those things. They are purely conceptual. They are ideas, phantoms, and ghosts. So, when you allow thinking to stop, all that goes away, and you find you're in an eternal here and now. There is no way you are supposed to be, and there is nothing you are supposed to do. There is no where you are supposed to go, because in order to think that you're supposed to do something you have to think.

It is incredibly important to un-think at least once a day for the very preservation of the intellectual life, because if you do nothing but think, as you're advised by IBM and by most of the academic teachers and gurus, you have nothing to think about except thoughts. You become like a university library that grows by itself through a process that in biology is called mitosis. Mitosis is the progressive division of cells into sub-cells, into sub-cells; so a great university library is very often a place where people bury themselves and write books about the books that are in there. They write books about books about books and the library swells, and it is like an enormous mass of yeast rising and rising, and that is all that is going on. It is a very amusing game. I love to bury my nose in ancient Oriental texts—it is fun, like playing poker or chess or doing pure mathematics. The trouble is that it gets increasingly unrelated to life, because the thinking is all words about words.

It we stop that temporarily and get our mind clear of thoughts, we become, as Jesus said, "again as children" and get a direct view of the world, which is very useful once you are an adult. There is not much you can do with it when you are a baby, because everybody pushes you around; they pick you up and sit you there. You can't do much except practice contemplation, and you can't tell anyone what it is like. But when, as an adult, you can recapture the baby's point of view, you will know what all child psychologists have always wanted to know—how it is that a baby feels. The baby, according to Freud at least, has the oceanic experience, that is to say, a feeling of complete inseparability from what's going on. The baby is unable to distinguish between the universe and his or her action upon the universe. Most of us, if we got into that state of consciousness, might be inclined to feel extremely frightened and begin to ask, "Who's in charge? I mean, who controls what happens next?" We would ask that, because we are used to the idea that the process of nature consists of controllers and controllees, things that do and things that are done to. This is purely mythological, as you find out when you observe the world without thinking, with a purely silent mind.

Now then, jnana yoga is the approach that is designed for intellectuals. There is an intellectual way to get to this kind of understanding. A lot of people say to me, "You know, I understand what you are talking about intellectually, but I don't really feel it. I don't realize it." I am apt to reply, "I wonder whether you do understand it intellectually, because if you did you would also feel it."

The intellect, or what I prefer to call the intelligence, is not a sort of watertight compartment of the mind that goes *clickety, clickety* all by itself and has no influence on what happens in all other spheres of one's being. We all know that you can be hypnotized by words. Certain words arouse immediately certain feelings, and by using certain words one can change people's emotions very easily and very rapidly. They are incantations, and the intellect is not something off over there. However, the word *intellect* has become a kind of catchword that represents the intellectual porcupinism of the academic world.

A certain professor at Harvard at the time Tim Leary was making experiments there said, "No knowledge is academically respectable which cannot be put into words." Alas for the department of physical education. Alas for the department of music and fine arts. That is very important, because one of the greatest intellects of modern times was Ludwig Wittgenstein. And as you read the end of his *Tractatus,* which was his great book, he shows you that what you always thought were the major problems of life and philosophy were meaningless questions. Those problems are solved not by, as it were, giving an answer to them but by getting rid of the problem through seeing intellectually that it is meaningless. Then you are relieved of the problem. You need no longer lie awake nights wondering what is the meaning of life, and what it is all about, simply because it isn't about anything. It's about itself, and so he ends up saying, "Whereof one cannot speak, thereof one must be silent."

A new successor to Wittgenstein, an Englishman named Spencer-Brown, has written a book called *Laws of Form,* and if any of you are mathematically minded I would firmly recommend it. He makes this comment about Wittgenstein: "True, there are certain things of which one cannot speak. For example, you cannot describe music." That is why most of the reports of music critics in the newspapers seem completely absurd. They are trying to convey in words how a certain artist performed, and they borrow words from all other kinds of art and try to make some show of being clever about it.

But there is no way in which the music critic, in words, can make you hear the sound of the concert. By writing certain instructions on paper telling you certain things to do, those sounds can be reproduced though, so musical notation is essentially a set of instructions telling you certain things to do, and if you do them, you will gain an experience that is ineffable and beyond words. Spencer-Brown points out that all mathematics is basically a set of instructions, like "describe a circle, drop a perpendicular." So, if you follow certain instructions, then you will understand certain things that cannot be described, and that, of course, is what yoga is all about.

All mystical writing, really, is instructions. It is not an attempt to describe the universe, to describe God, to describe ultimate reality. Every mystic knows that cannot possibly be done. The very word mysticism is from the Greek root *muin,* which means "silence." Mum's the word; shut up. I should talk, but that's it. Be quiet. Then you will understand because the instructions are to listen. Listen, or even look. Stop, look, and listen—that is yoga—and see what is going on. Only don't say, because that will spoil it. Somebody came to a Zen master and said, "The mountains and hills and the sky— are not all these the body of Buddha?" And the master said, "Yes, but it's a pity to say so."

For those of you who are mathematically hip, by reading Spencer-Brown's book *Laws of Form,* you can go through an intellectual process that is very close indeed to jnana yoga. As a matter of fact, I was so impressed with it that I went over to England especially to see this fellow. He is quite remarkable, a youngish man adept at all sorts of things.

In the book, he starts out with the instruction to draw a distinction, any distinction you want, between something and nothing, between the inside and the outside, or what have you. Then he takes you through a process of reasoning in which he shows you that once you have made that step, all the laws of mathematics, physics, biology, and electronics follow inevitably. He draws them out and he gets you into the most complicated electronic circuitry systems that necessarily follow from your having drawn a distinction. Once you have done that, the universe as we know it is inevitable.

After that he says, "I haven't told you anything you didn't already know. At every step when you saw that one of my theorems was correct, you said, 'Oh, of course.' Why? Because you knew it already." And then at the end of it, where he has shown you, as it were, the nature of your own mind, he raises the question, "Was this trip really necessary?"

So now he takes us in the reentry and says, "You see, what has happened through all this mathematical process, and also in the course of your own complicated lives where you have been trying to find out something that you already knew, is the universe has taken one turn." That is the meaning of *universe;* it has taken a turn on itself to look at itself. Well, when anything looks at itself it escapes itself, as the snake swallowing its tail, as the dog chasing its tail, as we try to grab this hand with that. It gets some of it, but it doesn't get it, and so he makes the amazing remark, "Naturally, as our telescopes become more powerful, the universe must expand in order to escape them." Now, you will say this is subjective idealism in a new disguise. This is Bishop Berkeley all over again saying that we create the universe out of our own minds. Well, unfortunately it is true, if you take *mind* to mean "physical brain" and "physical nervous system." If you listen to Karl Pribram's lectures at Stanford, you will find him saying the same thing in neurological terms. It is the structure of your nervous system that causes you to see the world that you see. Or read J. Z. Young's book *Doubt and Certainty in Science,* where all this is very clearly explained. It is the same old problem in new language, only it is a more complicated language, a more sophisticated, up-to-date, scientifically respectable language. It is the same old thing, but that is yoga. Yoga, or union, means that you do it. In a sense, you are God, *tat tvam asi,* as the Upanishads say, "You are making it."

So many spiritual teachers and gurus will look at their disciples and say, "I am God. I have realized." But the important thing is that you are realized. Whether I am or not is of no consequence to you whatsoever. I could get up and say "I am realized," and put on a turban and yellow robe and say "Come and have *darshan,*

I'm guru, and you need the grace of guru in order to realize," and it would be a wonderful hoax. It would be like picking your pockets and selling you your own watch. But the point is, you are realized. Now, what are we saying when we say that? We are obviously saying something very important, but alas and alack, there is no way of defining it, nor going any further into words about it. When a philosopher hears such a statement as *tat tvam asi,* "You are it," or "There is only the eternal now," the philosopher says, "Yes, but I don't see why you are so excited about it. What do you mean by that?"

Yet he asks that question because he wants to continue in a word game; he doesn't want to go on into an experiential dimension. He wants to go on arguing, because that is his trip, and all these great mystical statements mean nothing whatsoever. They are ultimate statements, just as the trees, clouds, mountains, and stars have no meaning, because they are not words. Words have meaning because they're symbols, because they point to something other than themselves.

But the stars, like music, have no meaning. Only bad music has any meaning. Classical music never has a meaning, and to understand it you must simply listen to it and observe its beautiful patterns and go into its complexity.

When your mind, that is to say, your verbal systems, gets to the end of its tether and it arrives at the meaningless state, this is the critical point. The method of jnana yoga is to exercise one's intellect to its limits so that you get to the point where you have no further questions to ask. You can do this in philosophical study if you have the right kind of teacher who shows you that all philosophical opinions whatsoever are false, or at least, if not false, extremely partial. You can see how the nominalists cancel out the realists, how the determinists cancel out the free willists, how the behaviorists cancel out the vitalists, and then how the logical positivists cancel out almost everybody. Then someone comes in and says, "Yes, but the logical positivists have concealed metaphysics," which indeed they do, and then you get in an awful tangle and there is nothing for you to believe.

If you get seriously involved in the study of theology and comparative religion, exactly the same thing can happen to you. You cannot even be an atheist anymore; that is also shown to be a purely mythological position. So you feel a kind of intellectual vertigo that is as in a Zen Buddhist poem, "Above, not a tile to cover the head. Below, not an inch of ground to stand on." Where are you then?

Of course, you are where you always were. You have discovered that you are it, and that is very uncomfortable because you can't grab it. I have discovered that whatever it is that I am is not something inside my head—it is just as much out there as it is in here. But whatever it is, I cannot get hold of it, and that gives you the heebie-jeebies. You get butterflies in the stomach, anxiety traumas, and all kinds of things. This was all explained by Shankara, the great Hindu commentator on the Upanishads and a great master of the non-dualistic doctrine of the universe, when he said, "That which knows, which is in all beings the knower, is never an object of its own knowledge." Therefore, to everyone who is in quest of the supreme kick, the great experience, the vision of God, whatever you want to call it—liberation—when you think that you are not it, any old guru can sell you on a method to find it. That may not be a bad thing for him to do, because a clever guru is a person who leads you on. "Here kitty, kitty, kitty, kitty. I've got something very good to show you. Yes. You just wait. Oh, but you've got to go through a lot of stages yet." You say "Ah, ah, ah, ah. Can I get that? Oh, I want to get that." And all the time it's you.

I was talking to a Zen master the other day, and he said, "Mmmmm. You should be my disciple." I looked at him and said, "Who was Buddha's teacher?" He looked at me in a very odd way, and he burst into laughter and gave me a piece of clover. So long as you can be persuaded that there is something more that you ought to be than you are, you have divided yourself from reality, from the universe, from God, or whatever you want to call that, the tat in tat tvam asi. You will find constantly, if you are interested in anything like this—in psychoanalysis, in Gestalt therapy, in sensitivity training, in any kind of yoga or what have you—that there will be that funny sensation of what I will call "spiritual greed" that can be aroused by somebody indicating to you, "Mmmm, there are still higher stages for you to attain. You should meet my guru." So, you might say, "Now, to be truly realized you have to get to the point where you're not seeking anymore." Then you begin to think, "We will now be non-seekers," like disciples of Krishnamurti, who because he says he doesn't read any spiritual books can't read anything but mystery stories, and become spiritually unspiritual. Well, you find that, too, is what is called in Zen "legs on a snake." It is irrelevant. You don't need *not* to seek, because you don't need anything. It is like crawling into a hole and pulling the hole in after you.

The great master of this technique was a Buddhist scholar who lived about 200 A.D. called Nagarjuna. He invented a whole dialectic, and he created *madhyamaka,* where the leader of the students would simply destroy all their ideas, absolutely abolish their philosophical notions, and they'd get the heebie-jeebies. He didn't have the heebie-jeebies. He seemed perfectly relaxed in not having any particular point of view. They said, "Teacher, how can you stand it? We have to have something to hang on to." "Who does? Who are you?" And eventually you discover, of course, that it is not necessary to hang on to or rely on anything. There is nothing to rely on, because you're it. It is like asking the question, "Where is the universe?" By that I mean the whole universe—whereabouts is it in space? Everything in it is falling around everything else, but there's no concrete floor underneath for the thing to crash on. You can think of infinite space if you like—you don't have to think of curved space, the space that goes out and out and out forever and ever and has no end: What is that? Of course, it is you. What else could it be? The universe is delightfully arranged so that as it looks at itself, in order not to be one-sided and prejudiced, it looks at itself from an uncountable number of points of view. We thus avoid solipsism, as if I were to have the notion that it is only me that is really here, and you are all in my dream. Of course, that point of view cannot really be disputed except by imagining a conference of solipsists arguing as to which one of them was the one that was really there.

Now, if you understand what I am saying by using your intelligence, and then take the next step and say, "I understood it now, but I didn't feel it," then next I raise the question, "Why do you want to feel it?" You say, "I want something more," but that is again spiritual greed, and you can only say that because you didn't understand it. There is nothing to pursue, because you are it. You always were it, and to put it in Christian terms or Jewish terms, if you don't know that you are God from the beginning, what happens is that you try to become God by force. Therefore you become violent and obstreperous and this, that, and the other. All our violence, all our competitiveness, all our terrific anxiety to survive is because we didn't know from the beginning that we were it.

Well, then you would say, "If only we did know from the beginning," as in fact you did when you were a baby. But then everybody says, "Well, nothing will ever happen." But it did happen, didn't it? And some of it is pretty messy. Some people say, "Well, take the Hindus. It is basic to Hindu religion that we are all God in disguise, and that the world is an illusion." All that is a sort of half-truth, but if that is the case—if really awakened Hindus by the knowledge of their union with the godhead would simply become inert, why then Hindu music, the most incredibly complex, marvelous technique? When they sit and play, they laugh at each other. They are enjoying themselves enormously with very complicated musical games. But when you go to the symphony everybody is dressed in evening dress and with the most serious expressions. When the orchestra gets up, the audience sits down, and it is like a kind of church. There is none of that terrific zest, where the drummer, the tabla player, laughs at the sarod player as they compete with each other in all kinds of marvelous improvisations. So, if you do find out, by any chance, who you really are, instead of becoming merely lazy, you start laughing. And laughing leads to dancing, and dancing needs music, and we can play with each other for a change.

INTRODUCTION
TO BUDDHISM

CHAPTER SIX

The idea of a *yana,* or vehicle, comes from the basic notion or image of Buddhism as a raft for crossing a river. This shore is ordinary everyday consciousness such as we have, mainly the consciousness of being an ego or a sensitive mind locked up inside a mortal body—the consciousness of being you in particular and nobody else. The other shore is release, or *nirvana,* a word that means literally "blow out," as one says, *whew,* in heaving a sigh of relief. Nirvana is never, never to be interpreted as a state of extinction or a kind of consciousness in which you are absorbed into an infinitely formless, luminous ocean that could best be described as purple Jell-O, but kind of spiritual. Horrors! It is not meant to be that at all. Nirvana has many senses, but the primary meaning of it is that it is this everyday life, just as we have it now, but seen and felt in a completely different way. Buddhism is called in general a *dharma*, and this word is often mistranslated as "the law." It is better translated as "the doctrine," and still better translated as "the method." The dharma was formulated originally by the Buddha, who was the son of a north Indian raja living very close to Nepal who was thriving shortly after 600 B.C. The word *buddha* is a title. The proper name of this individual was Gautama Siddhartha, and the word buddha means "the awakened one," from the Sanskrit root *buddh,* which means "to wake" or "to know." So, we could say buddha means "the man who woke up." The Buddha was a very skillful psychologist, and he is in a way the first psychotherapist in history, a man of tremendous understanding of the wiles and the deviousness of the human mind.

Buddhism is made to be easily understood. Everything is numbered so that you can remember it, and the bases of Buddhism are what are called the four noble truths. The first one is the truth about suffering, the second is the truth about the cause of suffering, the third is the truth about the ceasing of suffering, and the fourth is the truth about the way to the ceasing of suffering. So let's go back to the beginning—suffering. The Sanskrit word is *duhkha*. It means suffering in the widest possible sense, but "chronic suffering" or "chronic frustration" is probably as good a translation as any. Buddhism says the life of mankind and of animals— indeed also of angels, if you believe in angels—is characterized by chronic frustration. And so, that constitutes a problem. If any one of you says, "I have a problem"— well, I don't suppose you would be here if you didn't in some way have a problem—that is duhkha. Now, the next thing is the cause of it. The cause of it is called *trishna*. Trishna is a Sanskrit word that is the root of our word *thirst,* but means more exactly "craving," "clutching," or "desiring." Because of craving or clutching we create suffering, but in turn, this second truth is that behind trishna there lies another thing called ignorance—*avidya*, or "nonvisioned." *Vid* in Sanskrit is the root of the Latin *videre* and of our *vision*. And *a* in front of the word means "non." So, avidya is not-seeing, ignorance, or better, ig*nor*ance, because our mind as it functions consciously is a method of attending to different and particular areas of experience, one after another, one at a time.

When you focus your consciousness on a particular area, you ignore everything else. That is why to know is at the same time to ignore, and because of that, there arises trishna, or craving. Why? Because if you ignore what you really know, you come to imagine that you are separate from the rest of the universe, and that you are alone, and therefore you begin to crave or to thirst. You develop an anxiety to survive, because you think if you are separate, if you are not the whole works, you're going to die. Actually, you're not going to die at all. You are simply going to stop doing one thing and start doing something else.

When you die in the ordinary way, you just stop doing this thing, in this case called Alan Watts, but you do something else later. And there is nothing to worry about at all. Only when you are entirely locked up in the illusion that you are only this do you begin to be frightened and anxious, and that creates thirst. So, if you can get rid of ignorance (ig*nor*ance) and widen your mind out so as to see the other side of the picture, then you can stop craving. That does not mean to say you won't enjoy your dinner anymore, and that it won't be nice to make love, or anything like that. It doesn't mean that at all. It means that enjoying your dinner and making love, and generally enjoying the senses and all of experience, only become an obstacle to you if you cling to them in order to save yourself. However, if you do not need to save yourself, you can enjoy life just as much as ever: you don't have to be a puritan.

So, then, that is the state of letting go, instead of clinging to everything. Supposing you are in business and you have to make money to keep a family supported—that is the thing to do, but don't let it get you down. Do it, in what the Hindus call *nishkama karma*. *Nishkama* means "passionless" and *karma* means "activity." That means doing all the things that one would do in life, one's business, one's occupation, but doing it without taking it seriously. Do it as a game, and then everybody who depends on you will like it much better. If you take it seriously, they will be feeling guilty, because they will say, "Oh dear, Papa absolutely knocks himself out to work for us," and they become miserable. They go on, and they live their lives out of a sense of duty, which is a dreadful thing to do. So, that is nirvana, to live in a let-go way.

The fourth noble truth describes the way or the method of realizing nirvana, called the noble eightfold path. The eightfold path is a series of eight human activities, such as understanding or view, effort, vocation or occupation, speaking, conduct, and so forth, and they are all prefaced by the Sanskrit word *samyak*, which is very difficult to translate. Most people translate it as "right" in the sense of correct, but this is an incomplete translation. The root *sam* in Sanskrit is the same as our word *sum* through the Latin *summa*. The sum of things means completion, but it also conveys the sense of balanced or "middle-wayed." Buddhism is called the Middle Way, and we'll find out a great deal about that later.

Every Buddhist who belongs to the Theravada [or Hinayana] school in the south expresses the fact that he is a Buddhist by reciting a certain formula called tisarana and pancha-sila. I am talking Pali now, not Sanskrit. *Tisarana* means the three refuges, and *pancha-sila* means "the five precepts."

> *Buddham saddanam gacchame*
> *Dharmam saddanam gacchame*
> *Sangam saddanam gacchame*

That means "I take refuge in Buddha; I take refuge in the method, the dharma; I take refuge in the *sangha*" (which means the fraternity of the followers of Buddha). He then goes on to take the five precepts: "I promise to abstain from taking life," "I promise to abstain from taking what is not given," "I promise to abstain from exploiting my passions," "I promise to abstain from false speech," and "I promise to abstain from getting intoxicated" by a list of various boozes.

Now, every Buddhist in the Southern school says, "Mahayanists have a different formula." This is the method, and the method, the dharma, is therefore a moral law, but it isn't just like the Ten Commandments—it is quite different. You do not take the five precepts in obedience to a royal edict. You take them upon yourself, and there is a very special reason for doing so. How can you fulfill the precept not to take life? Every day you eat. Even if you're a vegetarian, you must take life. This is absolutely fundamental to an understanding of Buddhism. Buddhism is a method—it is not a doctrine. Buddhism is a dialogue, and what it states at the beginning is not necessarily what it would state at the end. The method of Buddhism is, first of all, a relationship between a teacher and a student. The student creates the teacher by raising a problem and going to someone about it.

Now, if he chooses wisely, he will find out if there is a buddha around to use as the teacher, and then he says to the buddha, "My problem is that I suffer, and I want to escape from suffering." So, the buddha replies, "Suffering is caused by desire, by trishna, by craving. If you can stop desiring then you will solve your problem. Go away and try to stop desiring." He then gives him some methods of how to practice meditation and to make his mind calm in order to see if he can stop desiring. The student goes away and practices this. Then he comes back to the teacher and says, "But I can't stop desiring not to desire. What am I to do about that?" So the teacher says, "Try, then, to stop desiring not to desire."

Now, you can see where this is going to end up. He might put it in this way: "All right, if you can't completely stop desiring, do a middle way. That is to say, stop desiring as much as you can stop desiring, and don't desire to stop any more desire than you can stop." Do you see where that's going to go? He keeps coming back because what the teacher has done in saying "Stop desiring" is he has given his student what in Zen Buddhism is called a *koan*. This is a Japanese word that means "a meditation problem," or more strictly, the same thing that *case* means in law, because koans are usually based on anecdotes and incidents of the old masters—cases and precedents. But the function of a koan is a challenge for meditation. Who is it that desires not to desire? Who is it that wants to escape from suffering?

Here we get into a methodological difference between Hinduism and Buddhism on the question of

"Who are you?" The Hindu says, "Your self is called the atman, the self. Now, strive to know the self. Realize I am not my body, because I can be aware of my body. I am not my thoughts, because I can be aware of my thoughts. I am not my feelings for the same reason. I am not my mind, because I can be aware of it. Therefore, I really am other than and above, transcending all these finite aspects of me."

Now, the Buddhist has a critique of that. He says, "Why do you try to escape from yourself as a body?" The reason is your body falls apart and you want to escape from it. "Why do you want to disidentify yourself from your emotions?" The reason is that your emotions are uncomfortable and you want to escape from them. You don't want to have to be afraid. You don't want to have to be in grief or anger, and even love is too much—it involves you in suffering, because if you love someone you are a hostage to fortune. So, the Buddha says the reason why you believe you are the *atman*, the eternal self, which in turn is the *brahman,* the self of the whole universe, is that you don't want to lose your damn ego. If you can fix your ego and put it in the safe-deposit box of the Lord, you think you've still got yourself, but you haven't really let go. So, the Buddha said there isn't any atman: he taught the doctrine of *anatman,* or nonself. Your ego is unreal, and as a matter of fact, there is nothing you can cling to—no refuge, really. Just let go. There is no salvation, no safety, nothing anywhere, and you see how clever that was. What he was really saying is that any atman you could cling to or think about or believe in wouldn't be the real one.

This is the accurate sense of the original documents of the Buddha's teaching. If you carefully go through it, that is what he is saying. He is not saying that there isn't the atman or the brahman, he's saying anyone you could conceive wouldn't be it. Anyone you believed in would be the wrong one, because believing is still clinging. There is no salvation through believing, there is only salvation through knowledge, and even then the highest knowledge is nonknowledge.

Here he agrees with the Hindus, who say in the *Kena Upanishad,* "If you think that you know Brahman, you do not know him. But if you know that you do not know the Brahman, you truly know." Why? It is very simple. If you really are it, you don't need to believe in it, and you don't need to know it, just as your eyes don't need to look at themselves. That is the difference of method in Buddhism. Now, understand "method" here. The method is a dialogue, and the so-called teachings of Buddhism are the first opening gambits in the dialogue. When they say you cannot understand Buddhism out of books, the reason is that the books only give you the opening gambits. Then, having read the book, you have to go on with the method. Now, you can go on with the method without a formal teacher. That is to say, you can conduct the dialogue with yourself or with life. You have to explore and experiment on such things as "Could one possibly not desire?" "Could one possibly concentrate the mind perfectly?" "Could one possibly do this, that, and the other?" And you have to work with it so that you understand the later things that come after trying these experiments. These later things are the heart of Buddhism.

So then, shortly after the Buddha's time, the practice of Buddhism continued as a tremendous ongoing dialogue among the various followers, and eventually they established great universities, such as there was at Nalanda in northern India. A discourse was going on there, and if you looked at it superficially, you might think it was nothing but an extremely intellectual bull session where philosophers were outwitting each other. Actually, the process that was going on was this: the teacher or guru in every case was examining students as to their beliefs and theories and was destroying their beliefs by showing that any belief that you would propose, any idea about yourself or about the universe that you want to cling to and make something of—use for a crutch, a prop, or a security—could be demolished by the teacher. This is how the dialogue works, until you are left without a thing to hang on to. Any religion you might propose, even atheism, would be torn up. They would destroy agnosticism and any kind of belief. They were experts in demolition, so they finally got you to the point where you had nothing left to hang on to. Well, at that point you are free, because you're it. Once you are hanging on to things, you put "it" somewhere else, something "I" can grab. Even when you think, as an idea, "Then I'm it," you are still hanging on to that, and so they are going to knock that one down.

So, when you are left without anything at all, you've seen the point. That's the method of the dialogue, essentially. That is the dharma, and all Buddhists make jokes about this. Buddha says in *The Diamond Sutra*, "When I attained complete, perfect, unsurpassed awakening, I didn't attain anything." Because to use a metaphor that is used in the scriptures, it's like using an empty fist to deceive a child. You say to a child, "What have I got here?" The child gets interested immediately and wants to find out, and you hide it. The child climbs all over you and can't get at your fist. Finally, you do let him get it, and there's nothing in it. Now, that is the method again. "Teacher, you have the great secret, and I know you have it. There must be such a secret somewhere somebody knows." And that secret is, "How do I get one up on the universe?" I don't know that I'm it, so

I'm trying to conquer it. So the teacher says, "Keep try-ing," and he gets you going and going and going and going—which shows you that in the end there is nothing to get, there never was any need to get anything and never was any need to realize anything, because you're it. And the fact that you think you're not is part of the game. So don't worry.

Many of the problems that are now being dis-cussed by modern logicians are, unbeknownst to them, already in the ancient Indian books: problems of seman-tics, of meaning, and of the nature of time and memory. All these were discussed with very, very meticulous scholarly sophistication, so it is my opinion that this was a very fertile period of human history, and that the phi-losophy in which it eventually emerged—the philosophy of Mahayana Buddhism—is as yet the most mature and really intelligent theory of human life and of the cosmos that man has ever devised. It is characteristic of this point of view that it adheres to the Middle Way, but the Middle Way does not mean moderation. It means the bringing together of opposites, of what we might call in our world spirit and matter, mind and body, mysticism and sensuality, unity and multiplicity, conformity and individualism. All these things are marvelously wedded together in the world view of Mahayana.

Fundamental to Mahayana Buddhism is the idea of what is called the *bodhisattva*. A bodhisattva is a per-son who has as his essence (*sattva*), *bodhi* (awakening). It is usually used to mean a potential buddha, someone who is, as it were, just about to become a buddha. That was the original sense, and part of the Pali canon is a book called the *Jatakamala,* the tales of the Buddha's previous lives—how he behaved when he was an animal and as a man long before he became Buddha. In all these stories, he is represented as sacrificing himself for the benefit of other beings, but since he had not yet become a fully fledged buddha, he is called in these stories a bodhisattva. That really means "a potential buddha," but the point is that as a potential buddha, as a bodhisattva, he is always involved in situations where he is feeding himself to the hungry tigers and so on.

Now, in the course of time, the term bodhisattva underwent a transformation. A bodhisattva matures and becomes a buddha, and what does that mean popularly? It means that whoever is fully awakened to the way things are is delivered from any necessity to be involved in the world anymore. In other words, you can go on to a transcendent level of being where time is abolished, where all times are now, where there are no problems, where there is perpetual eternal peace—nirvana in the sense of the word *parinirvana,* meaning beyond nirvana, super nirvana. So, if you are fed up with this thing and you don't want to play the game of hide-and-seek anymore, you can go into the parinirvana state and be in total serenity.

However, and again I am talking in the language of popular Buddhism, a person who stands on the threshold of that peace can turn back and say, "I won't be a buddha, I'll be a bodhisattva. I won't make the final attainment, because I would like to go back into the world of manifestation (called *samsara*) and work for their liberation." So, then, when a Mahayana Buddhist does his formula for *puja,* he says, "Sentient beings are numberless, I take a vow to save them. Deluding passions are inexhaustible, I take a vow to destroy them. The gates of the method, the dharma, are manifold, I take a vow to enter them. The Buddha way is supreme, I take a vow to complete it." Of course all this is impossible. Numberless sentient beings, because they are numberless, can never be delivered. Deluding passions which are inexhaustible can never be eradicated. So, this then is their formula.

The bodhisattva who returns into the world and becomes involved again is in fact regarded as a superior kind of being to the one who gets out of it. The person who gets out of the rat race and enters into eternal peace is called *pratyeka-buddha,* which means "private buddha," a buddha who does not teach or help others, and in Mahayana Buddhism that is almost a term of abuse. Pratyeka-buddha is a class with unbelievers, heretics, infidels, and fools, but the great thing is the bodhisattva.

All beings are thought of in popular Buddhism as constantly reincarnating again and again into the round of existence, helplessly, because they still desire. They are, therefore, drawn back into the cycle. The bodhisattva goes back into the cycle with his eyes wide open, voluntarily, and allows himself to be sucked in. This is normally interpreted as an act of supreme compassion, and bodhisattvas can assume any guise. They can get furiously angry if necessary in order to discourage evil beings, and could even assume the role of a prostitute and live that way so as to deliver beings at that level of life. They could become an animal, an insect, a maggot, or anything else, and all deliberately and in full consciousness to carry on the work of the deliverance of all beings. Now, that is the way the popular mind understands it.

Therefore, the bodhisattvas are all revered, respected, worshiped, and looked upon as we look upon God in the West—as saviors, as the Christian looks upon Jesus. Underneath this myth there is a profound philosophical idea going back to the Hindu philosophy of advaita and non-duality—namely, that the apparent dualism of "I" and "thou," of the knower and the known, the subject and the object, is unreal. So, also, the apparent duality between maya, the world illusion, and reality is unreal. The apparent duality or difference between the enlightened and the ignorant person is unreal. So, the apparent duality of bondage and deliverance, or liberation, is unreal. The perfectly wise man is the one who realizes vividly that the ideal place is the place where you are. This is an impossible thing to put in words. The nearest I could get to it would be to say that if you could see this moment that you need nothing beyond this moment—now, sitting here, irrespective of anything I might be saying to you, of any ideas you might have rattling around in your brains—here and now is the absolute "*which* in which there is no whicher." Only, we prevent ourselves from seeing this because we are always saying, "Well, there ought to be something more. Aren't I missing something somehow?" But nobody sees it.

Now then, the most far-out form of Mahayana Buddhism is called the Pure Land school, *Jodo-shin-shu*. *Jodo* means "pure land" and *shin-shu* means "true sect." This is based on the idea that there was in immeasurably past ages a great bodhisattva called Amitabha, and he made a vow that he would never become a buddha unless any being who repeated his name would automatically at death be born into the Pure Land over which he presides—that is, a kind of paradise. He did become a buddha, and so the vow works. All you have to do is repeat the name of Amitabha, and this will assure that without any further effort on your part you will be reborn into his western paradise when you die, and in that paradise, becoming a buddha is a cinch. There are no problems there. The western paradise is a level of consciousness, but it is represented in fact as a glorious place. You can see the pictures of it in Koya-san, wonderful pictures where the Buddha Amitabha is actually a Persian figure related to Ahura Mazda, which means "boundless light." The Daibutsu of Kamakura, that enormous bronze buddha in the open air, is *Amitabha.*

So, there he sits surrounded with his court, and this court is full of *upasaras,* beautiful girls playing lutes. And as you were born into the paradise, what happens when you die is you discover yourself inside a lotus, and the lotus goes *pop,* and there you find yourself sitting, coming out of the water, and here on the clouds in front of you are the upasaras sitting, strumming their lutes, with the most sensuous, beautiful faces.

Now, to get this, all you have to do is say the name of Amitabha. The formula is *Namu Amida butsu,* and you can say this very fast, "Namu Amida butsu, Namu Amida butsu, Numanda, Numanda, Numanda." When said many, many times, you are quite sure it is going to happen.

Actually, you only have to say it once, and you mustn't make any effort to gain this reward, because that would be spiritual pride. Your karma, your bad deeds, your awful past, is so bad that anything good you try to do is done with a selfish motive, and therefore doesn't effect your deliverance. Therefore, the only way to get deliverance is to put faith in the power of this Amitabha Buddha and to accept it as a free gift, and to take it by doing the most absurd things—by saying "Namu Amida butsu." Don't even worry whether you have to have faith in this, because trying to have faith is also spiritual pride. It doesn't matter whether you have faith or whether you don't, the thing works anyway, so just say "Namu Amida butsu." Now, that is the most popular form of Buddhism in Asia.

The two most vast temples in Kyoto, the initiant Higashi Honganji temples, represent this sect, and everybody loves Amitabha. *Amida,* as they call him in Japan—boundless light, infinite Buddha of Compassion, is sitting there with this angelic expression on his face: "It's all right, boys, just say my name, it's all you have to do." So when we add together prayer wheels, Namu Amida butsu (the Japanese call it *Nembutsu*) as the means of remembering Buddha, and all these things where you just have to say an abbreviated prayer and the work is done for you, wouldn't we Westerners, especially if we are Protestants, say, "Oh, what a scoundrelly thing that is, what an awful degradation of religion, what an avoidance of the moral challenge and the effort and everything that is required. Is this what the bodhisattva doctrine of infinite compassion deteriorates into?"

Now, there is a profound aspect to all that. Just as there is desperation and despair, nirvana desperation and despair of the horrors, so there are two ways of looking at this "nothing to do, no effort to make" idea, depending completely on the savior. For, who is Amitabha? Popularly, Amitabha is somebody else. He is some great compassionate being who looks after you. Esoterically, Amitabha is your own nature; Amitabha is your real self, the inmost boundless light that is the root and ground of your own consciousness. You don't need to do anything to be that. You are that, and saying Nembutsu is simply a symbolical way of pointing out that you don't have to become this, because you are it.

And Nembutsu, therefore, in its deeper side builds up a special kind of sage, which they called *myoko-nin*. Myoko-nin in Japanese means "a marvelous fine man," but the myoko-nin is a special type of personality who corresponds in the West to the holy fool in Russian spirituality, or to something like the Franciscan in Catholic spirituality.

I will tell you some myoko-nin stories because that is the best way to indicate their character. One day a myoko-nin was traveling and he stopped in a Buddhist temple overnight. He went up to the sanctuary where they have big cushions for the priests to sit on, and he arranged the cushions in a pile on the floor and went to sleep on them. In the morning the priest came in and saw the tramp sleeping and said, "What are you doing here desecrating the sanctuary by sleeping on the cushions and so on, right in front of the altar?" And the myoko-nin looked at him in astonishment and said, "Why, you must be a stranger here, you can't belong to the family."

In Japanese when you want to say that a thing is just the way it is, you call it *sonomama*. There is a haiku poem that says, "Weeds in the rice field, cut them down, sonomama, fertilizer." Cut the weeds, leave them exactly where they are, and they become fertilizer, or sonomama. And sonomama means "reality," "just the way it is," "just like that." Now, there is a parallel expression, *konomama*. Konomama means "I, just as I am." Just little me, like that, with no frills, no pretense, except that I naturally have some pretense. That is part of konomama. The myoko-nin is the man who realizes that "I, konomama—just as I am—am Buddha, delivered by Amitabha because Amitabha is my real nature." If you really know that, that makes you a myoko-nin, but be aware of the fact that you could entirely miss the point and become a monkey instead by saying, "I'm all right just as I am, and therefore I'm going to rub it in—I'm going to be going around parading my unregenerate nature, because this is Buddha, too." The fellow who does that doesn't really know that it's okay. He's doing too much, and he is coming on too strong. The other people, who are always beating themselves, are making the opposite error. The Middle Way, right down the center, is where you don't have to do a thing to justify yourself, and you don't have to justify not justifying yourself. So, there is something quite fascinating and tricky in this doctrine of the great bodhisattva Amitabha, who saves you just as you are, who delivers you from bondage just as you are. You only have to say "Namu Amida butsu."

It is fascinating, but that is the principle of Mahayana, and your acceptance of yourself as you are is the same thing as coming to live now, as you are. *Now* is as you are, in the moment, but you can't come to now, and you can't accept yourself on purpose, because the moment you do that you're doing something unnecessary. You are doing a little bit more. That is what they call in Zen putting legs on a snake or a beard on a eunuch. You've overdone it. How can you neither do something about it nor do nothing about it as if that was something you had to do? This is the same problem as originally posed in Buddhism: How do you cease from desiring? When I try to cease from desiring, I am desiring not to desire. Do you see this? All of this is what is called *upaya,* or skillful device, to slow you down so that you can really be here. By seeing that there is nowhere else you can be, you don't have to come to now. Where else can you be? It isn't a task or a contest—what the Greeks called *agone.* There is nowhere else to be, so they say, "Nirvana is no other than samsara." This shore is really the same as the other shore. As the *Lankavatara-sutra* says, "If you look to try to get nirvana in order to escape suffering and being reborn, that's not nirvana at all."

The philosophy of the *Tao* is one of the two great principle components of Chinese thought. There are, of course, quite a number of forms of Chinese philosophy, but there are two great currents that have thoroughly molded the culture of China—Taoism and Confucianism—and they play a curious game with each other. Let me start by saying something about Confucianism originating with K'ung Fu-tzu or Confucius, who lived a little after 630 B.C. He is often supposed to have been a contemporary of Lao-tzu, who is the supposed founder of the Taoist way. It seems more likely, however, that Lao-tzu lived later than 400 B.C., according to most modern scholars.

Confucianism is not a religion, it is a social ritual and a way of ordering society—so much so that the first great Catholic missionary to China, Matteo Ricci, who was a Jesuit, found it perfectly consistent with his Catholicism to participate in Confucian rituals. He saw them as something of a kind of national character, as one might pay respect to the flag or something like that in our own times. He found that Confucianism involved no conflict with Catholicism and no commitment to any belief or dogma that would be at variance with the Catholic faith. So, Confucianism is an order of society and involves ideas of human relations, including the government and the family. This order is based on the principle of what is called in Chinese *ren,* which is an extraordinarily interesting word. The word ren is often translated as "benevolence," but that is not a good translation at all. This word means "human-heartedness" (that's the nearest we can get to it in English), and it was regarded by Confucius as the highest of all virtues, but one that he always refused to define. It is above righteousness, justice, propriety, and other great Confucian virtues, and it involves the principle that human nature is a fundamentally good arrangement, including not only our virtuous side but also our passionate side—our appetites and our waywardness. The Hebrews have a term that they call the *yetzer ha-ra,* which means "the wayward inclination," or what I like to call the element of irreducible rascality that God put into all human beings because it was a good thing. It was good for humans to have these two elements in them. So, a truly human-hearted person is a gentleman with a slight touch of rascality, just as one has to have salt in a stew.

Confucius said the goody-goodies are the thieves of virtue, meaning that to try to be wholly righteous is to go beyond humanity and to be something that isn't human. So, this gives the Confucian approach to life, justice, and all those sorts of things a kind of queer humor, a sort of "boys will be boys" attitude, which is nevertheless a very mature way of handling human problems.

It was, of course, for this reason that the Japanese Buddhist priests (especially Zen priests) who visited China to study Buddhism introduced Confucianism into Japan. Despite certain limitations that Confucianism has—and it always needs the Taoist philosophy as a counterbalance—it has been one of the most successful philosophies in all history for regulation of governmental and family relationships. Confucianism prescribes all kinds of formal relationships—linguistic, ceremonial, musical, in etiquette, and in all the spheres of morals— and for this reason has always been twitted by the Taoists for being unnatural. But you need these two components, and they play against each other beautifully in Chinese society.

Roughly speaking, the Confucian way of life is for people involved in the world. The Taoist way of life is for people who get disentangled. Now, as we know in our own modern times, there are various ways of getting disentangled from the regular lifestyle of the United States. If you want to go through the regular lifestyle of the United States, you go to high school and college, and then you go into a profession or a business. You own a standard house, raise a family, have a car or two, and do all that jazz. But a lot of people don't want to live that way, and there are lots of other ways of living besides that.

So, you could say that those of us who go along with the pattern correspond to the Confucians. Those who are bohemians, bums, beatniks, or whatever, and don't correspond with the pattern, are more like the Taoists. Actually, in Chinese history, Taoism is a way of life for older people. Lao-tzu, the name given to the founder of Taoism, means "the old boy," and the legend is that when he was born he already had a white beard.

So, it is sort of like this: When you have contributed to society, contributed children and brought them up, and have assumed a certain role in social life, you then say, "Now it's time for me to find out what it's all about. Who am I ultimately, behind my outward personality? What is the secret source of things?" The later half of life is the preeminently excellent time to find this out. It is something to do when you have finished with the family business. I am not saying that is a sort of unavoidable strict rule. Of course, one can study the Tao when very young, because it contains all kinds of secrets as to the performance of every kind of art, craft, business, or any occupation whatsoever. In China, in a way, it plays the role of a kind of safety valve for the more restrictive way of life that Confucianism prescribes. There is a sort of type in China who is known as "the Old Robe." He is a sort of intellectual bum, often found among scholars, who is admired very much and is a type of character that had an enormous influence on the development of the ideals of Zen Buddhist life. He is one who goes with nature rather than against nature.

First of all, I am going to address ideas that come strictly out of Lao-tzu's book, the *Tao Te Ching*. Of course, the basis of the whole philosophy is the conception of Tao. This word has many meanings, and the book of Lao-tzu starts out by saying that the Tao that can be spoken is not the eternal Tao. You cannot give all the meanings, because the word tao means both "the way or course of nature or of everything" and "to speak." So, the actual opening phrase of the book, following this word tao, is a character that means "can be," or "can," or something like "able." So, according to its second meaning it is "the way that can be spoken, described, or uttered." But it also means the way that can be "wayed," although you would have to invent that word. The way that can be traveled, perhaps, is not the eternal way. In other words, there is no way of following the Tao; there is no recipe for it. I cannot give you any do-it-yourself instructions as to how it is done. It is like when Louis Armstrong was asked, "What is jazz?" He said, "If you have to ask, you don't know." Now that's awkward, isn't it? But we can gather what it is by absorbing certain atmospheres and attitudes connected with those who follow it. We can also gather what it is from the art, poetry, expressions, anecdotes, and stories that illustrate the philosophy of the way.

So, this word then, tao, the "way or the course of things," is not, as some Christian missionaries translated it, the Logos, taking as their point of departure the opening passage of Saint John's Gospel, "In the beginning was the word." If you look this up in a Chinese translation of the Bible, it usually says, "In the beginning was the Tao. And the Tao was with God, and the Tao was God. The same was in the beginning with God. All things were made by it and without it was not anything made that was made." So, they have substituted "Tao," and that would have a very funny effect on a Chinese philosopher, because the idea of things being made by the Tao is absurd. The Tao is not a manufacturer, and it is not a governor. It does not rule, as it were, in the position of a king. Although the book *Tao Te Ching* is written for many purposes, one of its important purposes is as a manual of guidance for a ruler. What it tells him is, essentially, "Rule by not ruling. Don't lord it over the people." And so, Lao-tzu says, "The great Tao flows everywhere, both to the left and to the right. It loves and nourishes all things, but does not lord it over them, and when good things are accomplished, it lays no claim to them." In other words, the Tao doesn't stand up and say, "I have made all of you. I have filled this earth with its beauty and glory. Fall down before me and worship." The Tao, having done everything, always escapes and is not around to receive any thanks or acknowledgment, because it loves obscurity. As Lao-tzu said, "The Tao is like water. It always seeks the lowest level, which human beings abhor." So, it is a very mysterious idea.

Tao, then, is not really equivalent with any Western or Hindu idea of God, because God is always associated with being the Lord. Even in India, the Brahman is often called the Supreme Lord, although that is a term more strictly applicable to Ishvara, the manifestation of Brahman in the form of a personal God. But the Lord Krishna's song is the *Bhagavad Gita,* the "Song of the Lord," and there is always the idea of the king and the ruler attached. This is not so in the Chinese Tao philosophy. The Tao is not something different from nature, ourselves, and our surrounding trees, waters, and air. The Tao is the way all that behaves. So, the basic Chinese idea of the universe is really that it is an organism. As we shall see when we get on to the *Chuang-tzu* (which was written by Chuang-tzu), who is the sort of elaborator of Lao-tzu, he sees everything operating together so that you cannot find the controlling center anywhere, because there isn't any. The world is a system of interrelated components, none of which can survive without the other, just as in the case of bees and flowers. You will never find bees in a place where there are not flowers, and you will never find flowers in a place where there are not bees or other insects that do the equivalent job. What that tells us, secretly, is that although bees and flowers look different from each other, they are inseparable. To use a very important Taoist expression, they arise mutually. "To be" and "not to be" mutually arise. This character is based on the picture of a plant, something that grows out of the ground. So, you could say, positive and negative, to be and not to be, yes and no, and light and dark arise mutually and come into being. There is no cause and effect; that is not the relationship at all. It is like the egg and the hen. The bees and the flowers coexist in the same way as high and low, back and front, long and short, loud and soft—all those experiences are experienceable only in terms of their polar opposite.

The Chinese idea of nature is that all the various species arise mutually because they interdepend, and this total system of interdependence is the Tao. It involves certain other things that go along with Tao, but this mutual arising is the key idea to the whole thing. If you want to understand Chinese and Oriental thought in general, it is the most important thing to grasp, because we think so much in terms of cause and effect. We think of the universe today in Aristotelian and Newtonian ways. According to that philosophy the world is separated. It is like a huge amalgamation of billiard balls, and they don't move until struck by another or by a cue. So, everything is going *tock, tock, tock,* all over the place; one thing starts off another in a mechanical way. Of course, from the standpoint of twentieth-century science, we know perfectly well now that this is not the way it works. We know enough about relationships to see that the mechanical model that Newton devised was all right for certain purposes, but it breaks down now, because we understand relativity and we see how things go together in a kind of connected net, rather than in a chain of billiard balls banging each other around.

So, then, we move to a second term that is extremely important. The expression *tzu-jan* is the term that we translate as "nature" in Chinese, but this term expresses a whole point of view. It does not say nature, *natura,* which means, in a way, "a class of things." It means, literally, "self so" or "what is so of itself." It is what happens of itself, and thus, spontaneity. Early on in the *Tao Te Ching,* Lao-tzu says, "The Tao's method is to be so of itself." Now, we might translate that as "automatic" were it not that the word *automatic* has a mechanical flavor. Tzu-jan, or *shizen* in Japanese, means "spontaneous": it happens as your heart beats. You don't do anything about it, don't force your heart to beat, and you don't make it beat—it does it by itself. Now, figure a world in which everything happens by itself—it doesn't have to be controlled, it is allowed. Whereas you might say the idea of God involves the control of everything going on, the idea of the Tao is of the ruler who abdicates and trusts all the people to conduct their own affairs, to let it all "happen." This doesn't mean that there is not a unified organism and that everything is in chaos. It means that the more liberty and the more love you give, and the more you allow things in yourself and in your surroundings to take place, the more order you will have.

It is generally believed in India that when a person sets out on the way of liberation, his first problem is to become free from his past karma. The word *karma* literally means "action" or "doing" in Sanskrit, so that when we say something that happens to you is your karma, it is like saying in English, "It is your own doing." In popular Indian belief, karma is a sort of built-in moral law or a law of retribution, such that all the bad things and all the good things you do have consequences that you have to inherit. So long as karmic energy remains stored up, you have to work it out, and what the sage endeavors to do is a kind of action, which in Sanskrit is called *nishkama karma*. Nishkama means "without passion" or "without attachment," and karma means "action." So, whatever action he does, he renounces the fruits of the action, so that he acts in a way that does not generate future karma. Future karma continues you in the wheel of becoming, samsara, the "round," and keeps you being reincarnated.

Now, when you start to get out of the chain of karma, all the creditors that you have start presenting themselves for payment. In other words, a person who begins to study yoga may feel that he will suddenly get sick or that his children will die, or that he will lose his money, or that all sorts of catastrophes will occur because the karmic debt is being cleared up. There is no hurry to be "cleared up" if you're just living along like anybody, but if you embark on the spiritual life, a certain hurry occurs. Therefore, since this is known, it is rather discouraging to start these things. The Christian way of saying the same thing is that if you plan to change your life (shall we say to turn over a new leaf?) you mustn't let the devil know, because he will oppose you with all his might if he suddenly discovers that you're going to escape from his power. So, for example, if you have a bad habit, such as drinking too much, and you make a New Year's resolution that during this coming year you will stop drinking, that is a very dangerous thing to do. The devil will immediately know about it, and he will confront you with the prospect of 365 drinkless days. That will be awful, just overwhelming, and you won't be able to make much more than three days on the wagon. So, in that case, you compromise with the devil and say, "Just today I'm not going to drink, you see, but tomorrow maybe we'll go back." Then, when tomorrow comes, you say, "Oh, just another day, let's try, that's all." And the next day, you say, "Oh, one more day won't make much difference." So, you only do it for the moment, and you don't let the devil know that you have a secret intention of going on day after day after day after day. Of course, there's something still better than that, and that is not to let the devil know anything. That means, of course, not to let yourself know. One of the many meanings of that saying "Let not your left hand know what your right hand doeth" is just this. That is why, in Zen discipline, a great deal of it centers around acting without premeditation. As those of you know who read Eugen Herrigel's book *Zen in the Art of Archery,* it was necessary to release the bowstring without first saying "Now." There's a wonderful story you may have also read by a German writer, Van Kleist, about a boxing match with a bear. The man can never defeat this bear because the bear always knows his plans in advance and is ready to deal with any situation. The only way to get through to the bear would be to hit the bear without having first intended to do so. That would catch him. So, this is one of the great problems in the spiritual life, or whatever you want to call it: to be able to have intention and to act simultaneously— this means you escape karma and the devil.

So, you might say that the Taoist is exemplary in this respect: that this is getting free from karma without making any previous announcement. Supposing we have a train and we want to unload the train of its freight cars. You can go to the back end and unload them one by one and shunt them into the siding, but the simplest of all ways is to uncouple between the engine and the first car, and that gets rid of the whole bunch at once. It is in that sort of way that the Taoist gets rid of karma without challenging it, and so it has the reputation of being the easy way. There are all kinds of yogas and ways for people who want to be difficult. One of the great gambits of a man like Gurdjieff was to make it all seem as difficult as possible, because that challenged the vanity of his students.

If some teacher or some guru says, "Really, this isn't difficult at all—it's perfectly easy," some people will say, "Oh, he's not really the real thing. We want something tough and difficult." When we see somebody who starts out by giving you a discipline that's very weird and rigid, people think, "Now there is the thing. That man means business." So they flatter themselves by thinking that by going to such a guy they are serious students, whereas the other people are only dabblers, and so on. All right, if you have to do it that way, that's the way you have to do it. But the Taoist is the kind of person who shows you the shortcut, and shows you how to do it by intelligence rather than effort, because that's what it is. Taoism is, in that sense, what everybody is looking for, the easy way in, the shortcut, using cleverness instead of muscle.

So, the question naturally arises, "Isn't it cheating?" When, in any game, somebody really starts using his intelligence, he will very likely be accused of cheating; and to draw the line between skill and cheating is a very difficult thing to do. The inferior intelligence will always accuse a superior intelligence of cheating; that is its way of saving face. "You beat me by means that weren't fair. We were originally having a contest to find out who had the strongest muscles. And you know we were pushing against it like this, and this would prove who had the strongest muscles. But then you introduced some gimmick into it, some judo trick or something like that, and you're not playing fair." So, in the whole domain of ways of liberation, there are routes for the stupid people and routes for the intelligent people, and the latter are faster. This was perfectly clearly explained by Hui-neng, the sixth patriarch of Zen in China, in his *Platform Sutra,* where he said, "The difference between the gradual school and the sudden school is that although they both arrive at the same point, the gradual is for slow-witted people and the sudden is for fast-witted people." In other words, can you find a way that sees into your own nature—that sees into the Tao immediately.

Earlier, I pointed out to you the immediate way, the way through now. When you know that this moment is the Tao, and this moment is considered by itself without past and without future—eternal, neither coming into being nor going out of being—there is nirvana. And there is a whole Chinese philosophy of time based on this. It has not, to my knowledge, been very much discussed by Taoist writers; it's been more discussed by Buddhist writers. But it's all based on the same thing. Zenji Dogen, the great thirteenth-century Japanese Zen Buddhist, studied in China and wrote a book called *Shobogenzo.* A *roshi* recently said to me in Japan, "That's a terrible book, because it tells you everything. It gives the whole secret away." But in the course of this book, he says, "There is no such thing as a progression in time. The spring does not become the summer. There is first spring, and then there is summer." So, in the same way, "you" now do not become "you" later.

In T. S. Eliot's *Four Quartets,* he says that the person who is settled down on the train to read the newspaper is not the same person who stepped onto the train from the platform. Therefore, you who sit here are not the same people who came in at the door: these states are separate, each in its own place. There was the "coming in at the door person," but there is actually only the "here-and-now sitting person." The person sitting here and now is not the person who will die, because we are all a constant flux. The continuity of the person from past through present to future is as illusory in its own way as the upward movement of the red lines on a revolving barber pole. You know it goes round and round, and the whole thing seems to be going up or going down, whichever the case may be, but actually nothing is going up or down. When you throw a pebble into the pond and you make concentric rings of waves, there is an illusion that the water is flowing outward, but no water is flowing outward at all. The water is only going up and down. What appears to move outward is the wave, not the water. So this kind of philosophical argument says that our seeming to go along in a course of time does not really happen.

The Buddhists say that suffering exists, but no one who suffers. Deeds exist, but no doers are found. A path there is, but no one follows it. And nirvana is, but no one attains it. In this way, they look upon the continuity of life as the same sort of illusion that is produced when you take a cigarette and whirl it in the dark and create the illusion of the circle, whereas there is only the one point of fire. The argument, then, is that so long as you are in the present there aren't any problems. The problems exist only when you allow presents to amalgamate. There is a way of putting this in Chinese that is rather interesting. They have a very interesting sign—it's pronounced *nin* (*nen* in Japanese). The top part of the character means "now" and the bottom part means "the mind heart," the *shin*. And so, this is, as it were, an instant of thought. In Chinese they use this character as the equivalent for the Sanskrit word *jnana*. Then, if you double this character and put it twice or three times, *nin, nin, nin*—it means "thought after thought after thought." The Zen master Joshu was once asked, "What is the mind of the child?" He said, "A ball in a mountain stream." He was asked, "What do you mean by a ball in a mountain stream?" Joshua said, "Thought after thought after thought with no block." He was using, of course, the mind of the child as the innocent mind, the mind of a person who is enlightened. One thought follows another without hesitation. The thought arises; it does not wait to arise. When you clap your hands, the sound issues without hesitation. When you strike flint, the spark comes out; it does not wait to come out. That means that there's no block.

So, "thought, thought, thought"—*nin, nin, nin*—describes what we call in our world the stream of consciousness. Blocking consists in letting the stream become connected, or chained together in such a way that when the present thought arises, it seems to be dragging its past, or resisting its future by saying, "I don't want to go." When the connection, or the dragging of these thoughts, stops, you have broken the chain of karma. If you think of this in comparison with certain problems in music it is very interesting, because when we listen to music, we hear melody only because we remember the sequence. We hear the intervals between the tones, but more than that, we remember the tones that led up to the one we are now hearing. We are trained musically to anticipate certain consequences, and to the extent that we get the consequences, we anticipate it, we feel that we understand the music. But to the extent that the composer does not adhere to the rules—and gives us unexpected consequences—we feel that we don't understand the music. If he gives us harmonic relationships that we are trained not to accept, or expect, we say, "Well this man is just writing garbage." Of course, it becomes apparent that the perception of music and the ability to hear melody will depend upon a relationship between past, present, and future sounds. You might say, "Well, you're talking about a way of living that would be equivalent to listening to music with a tone-deaf mind so that you would eliminate the melody and have only noise. In your Taoist way of life, you would eliminate all meaning and have only senseless present moments." Up to a point that is true; that is, in a way, what Buddhists also mean by seeing things in their suchness.

What is so bad about dying, for example? It's really no problem. When you die, you just drop dead, and that's all there is to it. But what makes it a problem is that you are dragging a past. And all those things you have done, all those achievements you've made and all these relationships and people that you've accumulated as your friends have to go. It isn't here now. A few friends might be around you, but all the past that identifies you as who you are (which is simply memory) has to go, and we feel just terrible about that. If we didn't, if we were just dying and that's all, death would not be a problem. Likewise, the chores of everyday life become intolerable when everything—all the past and future— ties together and you feel it dragging at you every way. Supposing you wake up in the morning and it's a lovely morning. Let's take today, right here and now—here we are in this paradise of a place and some of us have to go to work on Monday. Is that a problem? For many people it is because it spoils the taste of what is going on now. When we wake up in bed on Monday morning and think of the various hurdles we have to jump that day, immediately we feel sad, bored, and bothered. Whereas, actually, we're just lying in bed.

So, the Taoist trick is simply, "Live now and there will be no problems." That is the meaning of the Zen saying, "When you are hungry, eat. When you are tired, sleep. When you walk, walk. When you sit, sit." Rinzai, the great Tung dynasty master, said, "In the practice of Buddhism, there is no place for using effort. Sleep when you're tired, move your bowels, eat when you're hungry—that's all. The ignorant will laugh at me, but the wise will understand." The meaning of the wonderful Zen saying "Every day is a good day" is that they come one after another, and yet there is only this one. You don't link them. This, as I intimated just a moment ago, seems to be an atomization of life. Things just do what they do. The flower goes puff, and people go this way and that way, and so on, and that is what is happening. It has no meaning, no destination, no value. It is just like that. When you see that, you see it's a great relief. That is all it is. Then, when you are firmly established in suchness, and it is just this moment, you can begin again to play with the connections, only you have seen through them. Now they don't haunt you, because you know that there isn't any continuous you running on from moment to moment who originated sometime in the past and will die sometime in the future. All that has disappeared. So, you can have enormous fun anticipating the future, remembering the past, and playing all kinds of continuities. This is the meaning of that famous Zen saying about mountains: "To the naive man, mountains are mountains, waters are waters. To the intermediate student, mountains are no longer mountains, waters are no longer waters." In other words, they have dissolved into the point instant, the *tshana*. "But for the fully perfected student, mountains are again mountains and waters are again waters."

Alan
Watts
Audio
Collections

ON THE FOLLOWING PAGES are selected listings of
Alan Watts's most memorable performances recorded over a ten-year period.

USING STATE-OF-THE-ART technology, Electronic
University has captured and enhanced the natural
sound from the original recordings so that the
insights from one of this century's most notable
philosophers come through as clearly as the day he
spoke them.

ALAN WATTS AUDIO COLLECTIONS
Original Live Recordings
from Electronic University

The Tao of Philosophy — Volume I

❏ *Slices of Wisdom*—Notable segments drawn from the first thirteen weeks of the *Love of Wisdom* public radio series. (29 min.)

❏ *Images of God*—Watts explores the metaphysics underlying feminine symbolism in images of the divine throughout the world, in which "the deep" and "the dark" are recognized as the unifying ground of being. (29 min.)

❏ *Sense of Nonsense*—Recorded live on KPFA, this popular program is a delightful excursion into the essential purposelessness of life. (29 min.)

❏ *Coincidence of Opposites*—Just as the purpose of dancing is not to arrive at a certain place on the floor, life has no concrete goal to be achieved. (29 min.)

❏ *Seeing Through the Net*—In a sparkling 1969 talk to IBM systems engineers, Watts describes the "net" of perception we throw over reality, and the contrasting perceptions of "prickles" and "goo." (50 min.)

The Tao of Philosophy — Volume II

❏ *Myth of Myself*—What do we mean when we use the word "I"? Could self-image be the barrier to knowing who and what we really are? (42 min.)

❏ *Man and Nature*—Western culture sees the world as a mechanical system while Eastern philosophies see it as an all-encompassing organic process. Just as an apple tree "apples," the earth "peoples," and we are not so much born into this world as grown out of it. (56 min.)

❏ *Symbols and Meaning*—As symbols, words point to things they represent, and thus have meaning. By contrast, life itself does not stand for anything else, and therefore has no meaning in the usual sense. (29 min.)

❏ *Limits of Language*—Watts suggests that language may alter our view of reality, and by knowing the limits of language we can move on to the unspeakable. (29 min.)

The Philosophies of Asia — Volume I

❏ *The Relevance of Oriental Philosophy*—Alan Watts looks at Eastern thought in contrast with the religions of the Western world. Chinese and Indian models are used to point out how we can better understand our own culture by contrasting it with others. (56 min.)

❏ *The Mythology of Hinduism*—An engaging overview of the Hindu perspective on the universe, its theory of time, and the concept of an underlying godhead which is dreaming all of us. (54 min.)

❏ *Eco-Zen*—Speaking before a college audience, Watts points out that "ecological awareness" and "mystical experience" are different ways of saying the same thing. (29 min.)

❏ *Swallowing a Ball of Hot Iron*—Continuing an introduction toward the understanding of Zen Buddhism, Watts describes the essential unity of the organism and its environment. (29 min.)

The Philosophies of Asia — Volume II

❏ *Intellectual Yoga*—In a lively discussion of the intellect as a path to one's enlightenment, Watts observes that "it is amazing how many things there are that aren't so." (42 min.)

❏ *Introduction to Buddhism*—Buddhism is traced from its origins in India to China, and then on to Japan. Along the way Watts brings to life one of the world's great religious traditions in its many forms, from the Theravada school to contemporary Zen. (58 min.)

❏ *The Taoist Way of Karma I*—The word *karma* literally means "doing," and is thus "your doing" or action. Taoism suggests a spontaneous course of action in accord with the current and grain of nature. (29 min.)

❏ *The Taoist Way of Karma II*—By following the Tao, or course of nature, one comes into harmony with the world and drops out of the cycles of karma perpetuated by our attempts to control destiny. (29 min.)

EACH OF THE VOLUMES ABOVE consists of three audio cassettes in an attractive bookshelf binder. The price for each volume is $29.95. To order by phone, call (800) 969-2887. To order by mail, write to the address below. Please add $3 per item for shipping.

Electronic University
Post Office Box 2309
San Anselmo, CA 94979
(800) 969-2887

Also Available

❏ **Eastern & Western Zen**—Zen Stories (50 min);
Uncarved Block, Unbleached Silk (44 min.); Biting the Iron
Bull (45 min.); Swimming Headless (51 min.); Wisdom on
the Ridiculous (46 min.); Zen Bones (59 min.)

❏ **Buddhism**—The Journey from India (40 min.);
Following the Middle Way (42 min.); Buddhism as
Dialogue (62 min.); The Importance of Folly (58 min.);
Transcending Duality (47 min.); The Diamond Web
(40 min.)

❏ **Philosophy and Society**—On Time and Death
(50 min.); The Cosmic Drama (45 min.); Philosophy of
Nature (45 min.); What is Reality? (50 min.) Mysticism and
Morals (58 min.); On Being God (60 min.)

❏ **Myth and Religion**—Not What Should Be (60
min.); Spiritual Authority (55 min.); Jesus—His Religion
or the Religion About Him? (56 min.); Democracy in the
Kingdom of Heaven (50 min.); The Image of Man
(50 min.); Sex in the Church (52 min.)

Eᴀᴄʜ ᴏꜰ ᴛʜᴇ sɪx-ᴄᴀssᴇᴛᴛᴇ ᴀᴜᴅɪᴏ sᴇʀɪᴇs ᴀʙᴏᴠᴇ has its
own attractive bookshelf binder. The regular list price
for each series is $59.95. However, you may select
any two series for $100, any three for $140, or all
four for $175.

Please add $3 for priority mail per set, $10 per set for
overnight mail, or $5 per set for overseas shipping.
We accept Visa, MasterCard, and American Express
cards.

Electronic University
Post Office Box 2309
San Anselmo, CA 94979
(800) 969-2887